PRAISE FOR MICHAEL AARON ROCKLAND'S

NAVY

Rockland beautifully capt
military life—the humor, t
The stories are poignant and compelling, and Rockland's
recollections are a testament to how little has changed in
the military in the last fifty years.

Sergeant Matthew Lane
Iraqi Campaign combat veteran
U.S. Army, 2002-2010

This delightful and compelling memoir, written in a
polished style that is both witty and poignant, describes
events that occurred in the late 1950s in a locked
psychiatric ward at the U.S. Hospital at the Yokosuka
Naval Base in Japan. Rockland's experiences with the
Navy and with life in Japan are often reminiscent of my
own when I was stationed in Yokosuka. His experiences
as a medical corpsman were very different. The stories
of Navy and Marine mental patients are alternatively
frightening, sad, and, at times, bizarrely humorous. His
vivid tales portray life, death and madness where at one
moment all is placid and conventional and at the next
weirdly unpredictable, shocking, and even terrifying.
This is first-rate writing about a world that few of us have
ever seen or experienced, told with insight as well as
compassion.

Richard W. Wilson
Captain (Ret.) U. S. Naval Reserve

A memoir about a part of the Navy few are/were aware of, written with great humor. It can especially be enjoyed by those who may be familiar with a naval or other version of Ken Kesey's *One Flew Over the Cuckoo's Nest.*

Nick Romanetz, Colonel
United States Marine Corps (Ret.)

Most Navy men go to sea and many to war. Michael Aaron Rockland found himself ashore as a medic, tending to American sailor and marine mental patients in a locked psychiatric ward at a U.S. hospital in Japan where, though it was peacetime, he saw considerable "combat." His memoir is a very different kind of "war story," interesting for its look at the backwardness of military medicine in those days, especially in the treatment of gays, who were regarded not only as "sick" but as "criminals." The book explores the efforts of the Navy to constantly cover its tracks and to live by the code that "there is the right way, the wrong way, and the Navy way." Despite the book's serious concerns, it is also hilariously funny and a super-read.

Angus Kress Gillespie
Maritime Historian

In this riveting memoir, Michael Rockland takes us back to a time and place—a U.S. Naval psychiatric ward in Yokosuka, Japan in the mid-1950s—when gay sailors and marines were confined to a locked ward, along with murderers, to be treated for their "mental illness"—before being sent home to be confined at Leavenworth for their "criminality." This is a portrait of life in the Navy, years before even "don't ask, don't tell," that readers will not soon forget.

It has been said that you can't simultaneously wage war and seek peace, but on the N-2 locked psychiatric ward at Yokosuka Naval Base in Japan Navy medic, Michael Rockland, attempted to do both and remain sane under extremely dangerous conditions. Many decades removed, he returns to tell the story about a therapeutic community that operates "not the right way or the wrong way but the Navy Way." It is not a tale for the fainthearted.

Rockland's book is a combination *One Flew Over the Cuckoo's Nest* and *Catch- 22*. On the surface, it is about the Navy, but it is really about a young man's coming of age in the 1950s at a time when America was caught between World War II and the turbulent 1960s. He does it as a medical corpsman in a psychiatric ward with one guy who eats razor blades for lunch and two men who think they are Jesus. It is an eye opening and very funny look at both post-war America and post-war Japan, an emotional tour de force.

Other Works by Michael Aaron Rockland

Non-Fiction/ Scholarship

The George Washington Bridge: Poetry in Steel (2008)
The Jews of New Jersey: A Pictorial History (2001) (co-authored
   with Patricia M. Ard)
Popular Culture: Or Why Study Trash? (1999)
What's American About American Things? (1996)
Looking for America on the New Jersey Turnpike (1989) (co-
   authored with Angus Kress Gillespie)
Homes on Wheels (1980)
The American Jewish Experience in Literature (1975)
*America in the Fifties and Sixties: Julian Marias on the United
   States* (editor) (1972)
Sarmiento's Travels in the United States in 1847 (1970)

Non-Fiction/Memoir

An American Diplomat in Franco Spain (Spanish edition 2010,
   American edition 2012)
Snowshoeing Through Sewers (1994)

Fiction

Stones (2009)
A Bliss Case (1989)

Screenplay

Three Days on Big City Waters (1974) (co-authored with
   Charles Woolfolk)

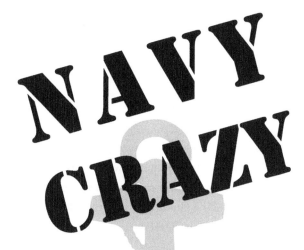

NAVY CRAZY

Michael Aaron
ROCKLAND

HP
G

HANSEN PUBLISHING GROUP

NORTHERN PLAINS
PUBLIC LIBRARY
Ault, Colorado

International Standard Book Number: 978-1-60182-298-7

Book and cover design by Jon Hansen

Hansen Publishing Group, LLC
302 Ryders Lane
East Brunswick, NJ 08816

http://hansenpublishing.com

For Sarah, Suwatana, and Joe

And for the two little guys who didn't make it into an earlier book,

Joey and Liam

When there is peace, the warlike man attacks himself.

—Friedrich Nietzsche

Contents

This is a memoir and is based on my life experiences. However, all names except mine are fictionalized, and any resemblance between the fictional names and any real person is strictly coincidental.

War Stories:
An Introduction

⚓

Men like to tell war stories. My war story took place during peacetime, but I did see combat. At the age of twenty, fresh out of college, just married to my eighteen year old girlfriend—young, naïve, and insecure, an intellectually minded kid in glasses—I was drafted into the Navy. But I never set foot on a ship, never fired a weapon. My combat was with guys on our side.

What I did was work as a hospital corpsman or medic or "pecker checker" as we were familiarly called: somebody had the clap, you gave them a penicillin shot in the butt. Only, gonorrhea wasn't a major issue on the locked psychiatric ward for United States Navy and Marine mental patients in Japan where I worked.

Marines were also our patients because, though essentially a separate branch, they don't have their own medical corps. They also remain under the Department of the Navy—technically, soldiers aboard ships. The word "marine," after all, refers to the sea, and marines have always been adept at amphibious landings. I'm sure most Navy and Marine personnel, then and now, are reasonably normal, reasonably sane, but, given the peculiarities of my assignment, I didn't meet many. Most military personnel I knew during my year-and-a-half in Japan were crazy. And nothing would have made some of them happier than to kill me.

I worked at the hospital on the United States Naval Base in Yokosuka, once a formidable Japanese facility, then and now the largest U.S. naval base in the Far East. Since my years in the Navy were 1955 to 1957, after Korea and before Vietnam, the large wooden firetrap of a hospital, built by the Japanese in 1931, was almost empty; there were no wounded. The medics on the other wards mostly sat around playing cards, but the psychiatric wards were overflowing.

I've often wondered: could there be as much, if not more, mental illness in the military during peacetime as during wartime, another kind of PTSD, *Pre*-Traumatic Stress Disorder? Or to put it another way, is it possible that some of our patients were so hungry for war they could have used a little trauma?

I have met war veterans who say shooting people and being shot at was the highlight of their lives. Not falling in love. Not getting married. Not fathering children. One vet told me, "Combat is the greatest rush. Better than sex."

Many of the patients on our ward were guys who had re-upped after finishing their first tour. Briefly at home, they were bored, missed the excitement and the danger. Also, after years under military discipline, always told what to do, they were ill-equipped for freedom's uncertainties.

Such men reminded me of penitentiary inmates who, once released, quickly commit a crime so they could be sent back to a place where all choice is out of their hands. After facing life "on the outside," returning to the Navy or Marines can be a comfort and re-upping a kind of recidivism.

If there was a typical patient on our ward it was a veteran of the Korean War now stationed in Japan, bored, with nothing to do. This was back when "Made in Japan" was a joke and everything was unbelievably inexpensive. Off the base in Yokosuka city a decent looking woman cost about a buck in yen, and you could shoot up with heroin in an alley for even less in Japanese currency. You could also get a bottle of Cutty Sark for $1.25 at the base Post Exchange (PX). Some of these guys had been doing all three round the clock before they lost it and ended up on our ward. But with no war, no one to shoot, some of them had strangled their Japanese girlfriends or slashed their wrists or shot another sailor or marine.

A much decorated marine patient on our ward once said to me, "I loved it in Korea. I was somebody. Here in Japan I'm shit. They won't even let me carry my .45 off base." He had little sympathy for the treaty, implemented in 1952, stipulating that while the United States could maintain bases in Japan, it was no longer an occupier power. "We shoulda occupied these sneaky sumbitches forever," he said.

This marine said that if and when he left the military he planned to become a policeman. If he had to be a civilian, he wanted a job where he could carry a gun. I hope he never was allowed to become a cop; he would have been a menace. For years afterward I sometimes searched the faces of policemen wherever I went hoping never to see his. If a war had broken out, our ward could have released some excellent killers, and it wouldn't have surprised me if, once on the battlefield, they immediately went sane.

We had two psychiatric wards, N-1 and N-2. N-1 was the open ward, N-2 the locked. All patients were initially admitted through N-2, the dark, prison-like place where I worked. The Japanese had used it during World War II for military personnel jailed for crimes who needed medical attention.

N-2 was about 120 feet long and 35 wide, not much larger than a stage set. Indeed, as I look back on it now I sometimes think of the ward as a theater. Everything happening there was dramatic and, being so contained, explosive.

The ward was crammed with thirty patients, most of the space occupied by their double decker steel racks. "Racks" are what beds are called in the Navy. Even in the locked psychiatric ward there was the pretense that we were aboard ship. The floor was "the deck." The bathroom was "the head." The walls were "bulkheads."

N-2 resembled the inside of a submarine—everything locked down, iron cages on the windows, steel doors. Not exactly a dungeon, but close. If you weren't crazy when you got there you might soon be. Sheer claustrophobia would have been sufficient. The patients were in there 24-7; I was there for only 8 hour shifts, but, when going off duty each day, I took a deep breath and could feel my heart slowing down.

The only ways out of the ward were the heavy front and back doors, and the back door led to the recreation yard, which was surrounded by a fifteen foot fence topped by barbed wire. We medics carried the keys to the ward on brass holders fastened to the belt loops on our pants.

They had a locking device so patients couldn't grab them without tearing off one side of our bell bottoms.

On N-2, the shrinks would see newly admitted patients as quickly as possible and the great majority would be shipped upstairs to N-1 which, unlike N-2, was large and airy, with light streaming in through the windows. Often N-1 guys flipped after receiving a "Dear John" letter from their girlfriends, or maybe they were just lonely or in culture shock from dealing with Japanese ways—all that bowing, all that smiling, all those surgical masks obscuring the faces of people, as if there was an epidemic in the streets.

As N-1 patients improved, their freedoms were increased. First, they were allowed to go anywhere in the hospital, then anywhere on the base. Finally, they were granted liberty and went into Yokosuka town and got laid. After that they were ready to return to duty.

Serious patients, Section 8s, were kept on our locked ward and almost all of them were eventually air-evacuated back to the United States, some into Veterans Administration hospitals, others court-martialed and sent to prison.

We had five classes of patients on our ward. We had murderers—there to be observed by the psychiatrists before they testified at their trials. We had suicides—guys who hadn't quite managed to off themselves, usually cutting both wrists. We had "whackjobs" or "looneys"—schizophrenics or paranoids who babbled and hallucinated or thought they were Jesus, Moses, or the King of Siam. We had catatonics—"cats" or "veggies"—guys who just sat there, so you had to feed them and dress them and try to anticipate when to get them to the bathroom so they didn't shit themselves because, if they did, you had to clean them. And this being the 1950s, we had "faggots," who were considered not only sick but "criminals." They were among those who usually got court-martialed when they left us and ended up in Leavenworth for a couple of years.

I want the reader to understand my use of such words as "faggot," "whackjob," "looney," "cat," and "veggie" throughout this book. I have not used such words since my days on N-2. But to help capture the ward's atmosphere, its flavor, its culture—and to be accurate—I use the language used there.

Striving for accuracy in a war story is especially important because there is a natural tendency to exaggerate. Also, the reader may wonder with what accuracy one can report on events so long ago. Memory, even following events that took place in the immediate past, can be tricky. One remembers what one chooses to remember. And one's memories are conditioned not only by who one was but by who one has become. Thus, a memoir is perhaps as much about a writer's mind and its evolution as about the story told. Others who worked on N-2 when I did might remember things differently. No, they would *definitely* remember things differently; everyone remembers things differently. Thus, while a memoir is non-fiction, it is a very subjective form of non-fiction because the minds and memories of no two observers and no two writers are the same.

Complicating issues of memory, there have recently been a number of scandals in the literary world involving memoirists and other, supposedly non-fiction writers who made up their own stories. That I know of, I have made nothing up except names to protect the innocent, the guilty, and everyone in-between. But, in a sense, "all writing is fiction," as I have said in another book. "It's just that some writing is more 'fictional' than other writing."

Some would say this is academic, post-modern nonsense, typical of a guy who has spent much of his life teaching at a university. Nah, I just wanted to share with the reader that telling the slippery truth, especially in a war story, isn't always easy.

Billy

Billy Goldsmith was admitted to N-2 shortly after I began working there—while I was still idealistically committed to helping patients.

Billy was different from the other patients. I couldn't see anything wrong with him. He seemed to be the sanest person on the ward—and I'm including the staff here: the two psychiatrists, the psychologist, the nurse, and us, the medics.

Billy didn't seem even a tad neurotic. He was, for me, an oasis of sanity in the nut ward. He was a towheaded kid from Kansas who looked like the all-American boy and acted like him too. And he was smart. Whenever I had a minute—the murderers weren't threatening anyone, the suicides were calm, the whackjobs were under control, the catatonics were already fed and hadn't shit themselves, and the faggots were all in plain sight—we were told by Captain Quarter, the head shrink, never to take our eyes off the faggots lest they "try to climb up someone's back"—I'd pull up a chair and go sit with Billy by his rack.

Billy and I would talk about literature and art. He said he wanted to be a writer, so we had that in common. Being friendly with patients wasn't prohibited. In fact, the mantra on our ward was that we were "a therapeutic community," so being friendly with the patients was encouraged. Once a day, for an hour and a half, we had a group therapy session at the back of the ward. Not much was accomplished. The murderers were sullen; they didn't know whether, when they left our ward, they would get off on an insanity plea, were going to jail for life, or might even be hung. Depending on whom they had killed, they would be tried by an American military court or by a Japanese court.

The suicides didn't say much either, just sat there waving their hands around with those big white bandages on their wrists and hands, like taped boxers who hadn't yet put on their gloves. And, of course, the catatonics didn't say anything. The whackjobs had much to say but it was often gibberish. The homosexuals had a lot to say too, but someone, usually a murderer, was likely to silence them by saying, "Shut up, faggot." So the daily group therapy session wasn't very—well—therapeutic.

Still, we were constantly told to "treat these guys like human beings," even the faggots. I say "even" because, within the ward, homosexuals occupied the lowest station, even below that of the murderers.

I certainly treated Billy like a human being. And it was easy, because I genuinely liked the kid. When not talking to me, Billy read—not comic books like most guys in the Navy and Marines, but Fitzgerald, Faulkner, Twain, Steinbeck. I couldn't figure out why Billy was classified as a Section 8. Okay, maybe he was too slim, but if I was any judge of character at all, he was no section anything.

So what was he doing on our locked ward? There was absolutely nothing wrong with him. I didn't think he even belonged on the open ward or in the hospital at all. This was, I was sure, just another Navy screwup. Someone had made a mistake—either a shrink at Billy's unit or the shrinks on our ward, maybe both. SNAFU as they said: "Situation Normal All Fucked Up." They'd meant to send somebody else to our ward and sent Billy by mistake. With each passing day I became more convinced that something had to be done about Billy and, if nobody else was going to, I would.

Did Billy share my feelings about his presence on our ward? I asked him: "Hey, Bill, what have they got you in here for?" I hadn't even bothered to look at his chart, so convinced was I that Billy had nothing wrong with him.

"Haven't a clue," he replied, but he didn't seem angry about it, appeared perfectly content. "This is great duty," he said. "No work, can read all I want, nobody telling me what to do. It's like a resort." He had a point—but didn't giving up his freedom mean anything to him?

"You know, Billy," I said to him one day when we were talking about literature, "you remind me a little of Melville's Billy Budd."

He laughed; he'd read most of Melville. "Maybe I look like him," he said, "but nobody's persecuting me."

One night, when I was off duty and sleeping in the barracks, I dreamed about Billy. In the dream I engineered his escape from the locked ward. When one of those large, wheeled laundry carts came onto the ward, fresh linen on top, I stood over it, blocking the view of anyone looking that way, and Billy climbed in the bottom and I covered him up with outgoing, soiled linen. When they got the cart down to the laundry and no one was attending it, Billy jumped out, took off his pajamas, and snagged a Navy uniform off a hanger. He made it off the base and out of Japan. I woke up when a postcard arrived from Kansas saying how happy he was to be back in "the land of the big PX," code for America.

That same day, before going on duty in the locked ward (I was on the p.m. shift then, 3:00-11:00). I went to see Captain Quarter, the chief shrink. He was in charge of both wards, but his office was upstairs in the open ward. I hoped to convince Quarter that Billy didn't belong on our ward.

Quarter, who looked like not only his uniform but his whole body was starched, was watering his plants; he always seemed to be watering his plants. "Captain," I said, pausing in his doorway, "permission to speak to you about one of our patients."

"Yeah," he said, his mustache twitching, "what's this about, Rockhead?"

"Rockland, Sir."

"Yeah, whatever," Quarter said, suggesting that getting my name straight was of little importance to him. Quarter never did get my name straight. I always wondered whether this was a mistake or his way of keeping me in my place, given the cavernous separation between his rank and mine.

I told Quarter about Billy. "Sir," I said, "with all due respect. I think a mistake has been made. I don't think there's anything the matter with Petty Officer Third Class, William Goldsmith."

Quarter stopped watering his plants and stared at me. "You a psychiatrist, Rockhead?"

"No sir," I said.

"Then what makes you think you can diagnose patients?"

"I don't think that, Sir," I said. "It's just that I know this kid. He's absolutely normal."

Quarter put down his watering can and stared at me hard. "Rockhead," he said, "No one is kept on the locked ward without a regular review of his case. Now, get out of my face; this is getting very close to insubordination."

"But…" I started to say something but then thought better of it. "Sir," I said, saluted, and headed downstairs to the locked ward.

I happened to be talking with Billy Goldsmith when the food cart came onto the ward with dinner at 5:30. Most of the other patients got on line. Billy just sat there. I had to feed one of the catatonics but, before doing so, I said to Billy, "Aren't you going to get some dinner?"

"Not hungry," he said.

At the time I gave this little importance. I figured Billy must have squirreled away a candy bar when the canteen cart came on the ward the previous night. And, besides, no one on the locked ward had much of an appetite since they mostly sat around all day.

But the next evening the food cart came on the ward and, while feeding one of the catatonics, I noticed that Billy didn't get up this time either. That was strange. Surely, he must be hungry tonight if he wasn't last night.

Later on I sat with Billy for a few minutes and said, "Not hungry again tonight?'

"Not a bit," he said. "I've had tons to eat today."

The following evening the same thing happened. Billy didn't get up when the food cart came on the ward, and when I inquired he again said that he had had plenty to eat that day.

I didn't want to be questioning someone I considered a friend, but I asked, "What'd you have?

"Coffee," he said.

"Just coffee?" I asked

"Well," he said, "lots of coffee."

"How many cups?" I asked.

"About sixty." There was a large coffee machine on the ward which one medic on each shift was responsible for keeping full. Patients and staff could help themselves to it at any time. Come to think of it, Billy often had a cup of coffee in his hand when we talked. I had never before paid attention to this, but now I was. Sixty cups of coffee a day?! But I didn't drink coffee then—it tasted awful to me—and didn't understand why anyone did, so although sixty sounded like a lot, I wasn't as alarmed as I might have been.

"How do you take it, Billy," I asked hopefully, "cream and sugar?" I figured that at least if he took his coffee with cream and sugar he was getting some nourishment.

"Nah," he said, "I like it black."

"Black?!" I said, astounded, thinking this might explain how slim he was. Only I wasn't thinking "slim" any more, I was thinking "skinny." Sixty cups of black coffee a day?" I asked. "Doesn't it give you the shakes? Can you sleep at night?"

"Oh," he said, casually, "I don't need much sleep."

"Well," I asked, "how much sleep do you get?"

"Maybe once every four or five nights I sleep."

"Once every four or five nights?!" I asked. "What do you do the rest of the nights when the lights go out at 11:00?"

"I think," he said, pushing his blond bangs back from his eyes.

"You just lie there and think?"

"Well, no," he said laughing. "I also spank the monkey."

"Spank the monkey?" This was a new term for me.

"Yeah, you know: jerk off."

"None of my business," I said, "but how often do you do that?"

"Oh, eight or nine times a night. Sometimes more."

With what he was eating I wondered that he had the energy, quite apart from the fact that so much masturbating would, I thought, give you a pretty sore penis. At the same time, I wondered if I was somehow deficient. Once had always been enough for me.

"And you don't eat anything but sixty cups of black coffee a day?"

"Oh, no," he said. "I have plenty more to eat."

"Like what?" I asked

"Cigarettes," he said. "I smoke a lot of cigarettes."

"Like how many?"

"Oh, five or six packs a day." Only then did I realize that whenever Billy and I were talking, he not only had a cup of coffee in one hand but a cigarette in the other. And there always seemed to be open cigarette cartons on his yellow metal nightstand and an ashtray full to overflowing.

I hadn't paid any attention to Billy's smoking because most of the patients on the ward smoked. So did some of the staff. Every night, around nine o'clock, the canteen cart came on the ward with cigarettes, candy, gum. But five or six packs a day? Even by the 1950s there was talk about cigarettes and lung cancer despite such ads as, "More Doctors Smoke Camels" and the one for Old Gold, "Not A Cough In A Carload." There was no talk then about second hand smoke. People smoked throughout the hospital, except in the operating rooms, and that was only because of the oxygen.

"What else do you 'eat' Billy?" I asked.

"Nothing else," he said. "With all that coffee and those cigarettes, I'm stuffed. I couldn't eat another thing."

Jeez, I thought. No wonder Billy's so skinny. Only now I wasn't thinking skinny; I was thinking emaciated. And in addition to all that black coffee and cigarettes, he must be wearing himself out with the masturbating. But I still didn't think Billy was crazy or anything, just different. He was too normal to be crazy, whatever Captain Quarter thought. Naively, I decided to help him on the dietary front; then he'd be fine.

"Billy," I said, "you and me are pretty good friends, aren't we?"

"Oh, you're the best friend I've ever had," Billy said. "Best friend" sounded a bit strong. Billy and I were friends, but best friends ever? I'd only known him two weeks; I felt under a certain pressure. Maybe it was wrong of me to have gotten that friendly with him. Could a patient really be your friend? Of course, I'd never really thought of Billy as a patient before.

"So, Billy," I said, "since we're such good friends I wonder if you would do me a favor."

"Sure, Mike," he said, "anything."

"Billy, when I come on duty for the p.m. shift tomorrow I want you to have eaten something besides the coffee and the cigarettes. Would you do that for me? I know you might be stuffed with the coffee and cigarettes, but would you eat something when the lunch cart comes on the ward? And when the dinner cart comes on the ward I'll be here and I can watch you eat. It would really make me happy. Would you do that for me as a favor—you know, in honor of our friendship?"

"Sure, Mike," Billy said. "It will be my pleasure. When you come on the ward tomorrow I'll tell you exactly what I ate at lunchtime. And then maybe I'll have some more at dinner."

"Thanks, Billy," I said, and I meant it. Working in the locked ward offered few pleasures. You wanted to occasionally feel you had made progress with a patient—you weren't just his "keeper." And if I could do that with Billy, who I liked so much—perhaps even set him on the road to getting out of the ward —it would be especially satisfying.

I looked forward to returning to work the next afternoon and getting the good news from Billy. When I came on the ward, he was waiting for me with a big smile. Before I could say anything, he offered, "I ate something besides the coffee and cigarettes today, Mike. I hope you'll be pleased."

"Wonderful," I said, "What did you eat?

"Razor blades," Billy said.

"Razor blades?!" I repeated, stunned. "You're joking, right?"

"No," Billy said. "You're my friend, Mike. I wouldn't joke with you. I figured I might be a little anemic with just the coffee and cigarettes. Lots of iron in razor blades."

This was before throwaway razors. Two sided razor blades had to be inserted. But, for two reasons, I didn't believe Billy. First, we kept razor blades locked up. Patients didn't shave themselves; the a.m. crew shaved half the patients each day, so patients got shaved every other day. But not only were razor blades kept locked up; those being used were placed in razors fastened from below with a tool that was also kept under lock and key. There was no way to get blades out without that tool. How could Billy have gotten hold of razor blades?

I thought I would humor him; this was probably just a fantasy. "How many razor blades did you eat?" I asked.

"I hope you don't mind, Mike," he said, "only four. I saved a few more for dinner, so you could watch me eat like you said." He opened his bedside table drawer, where there were four more blades. I quickly shut the drawer before other patients could see them.

"But how could you swallow razor blades?" I said— the second reason why I didn't believe him. "That's impossible."

"Not if you break them in half, "Billy said with a big smile. "I ate eight halves. Lots of iron, like I said."

"Billy, tell me you're joking," I said, beginning to panic. If he had really done this he was going to die. If they hadn't already, those razor blades would cut him to pieces inside. He would bleed to death.

"Mike," he said, "true friends always tell each other the truth."

I still didn't believe him but I had to do something. I told Kreeg there were four razor blades in Billy's drawer and that I had to leave the ward for a few minutes to see Captain Quarter about Billy.

"What about?" Kreeg said.

"Tell you later," I said, "but get the blades, okay?" I ran upstairs to the open ward and sheepishly knocked on Quarter's door.

"On the phone," he yelled, "be with you soon."

Soon? What was "soon?" If Billy had swallowed those razor blades "soon" might not be soon enough. And if he had eaten them, he had done so to please me; it was my fault.

Time passed. From the little I could hear through the door Quarter seemed to be having a conversation with somebody about going bowling; there was a bowling alley on the base.

I knocked on the door again. "Sir, "I yelled, "I think we have an emergency."

After a minute or so Quarter opened the door. The phone was off the hook on his desk, so he apparently hadn't finished talking about the bowling. "This better be good Rockhead," he said. I had gotten used to not correcting him.

"Sir," I said, "Goldsmith, that patient on the locked ward I once spoke with you about, says he ate four razor blades, eight halves."

"You gotta be kidding," Quarter said. "How could he get ahold of razor blades?"

"I don't know, Sir," I said. "He said he ate them before I came on duty for the p.m. shift." I thought it best not to mention the four blades in Billy's drawer. Kreeg had certainly recovered them by now.

"And this is the patient you told me is so normal he doesn't belong on the locked ward, the open ward, or any other ward?"

"I'm afraid so, Sir."

"Well, he's probably bullshitting you, but we can't take a chance. Get that son-of-a-bitch down to X-ray. Simon from the open ward will go with you. We can't spare anyone else from N-2."

He yelled into the open ward: "Simon, come here." I was glad to have Jerry Simon going with me. Though we'd gone through boot camp and hospital corpsman's school together, we didn't see much of each other now. Working on different wards and almost always on different shifts, we were rarely off duty at the same time. It was a pity because he was someone I could talk to.

"Okay, Rockhead," Quarter said, "you and Simon get that kid down to X-ray immediately. I'll phone ahead and tell them you're coming. Understood?"

"Understood, Sir," I said. Jerry and I ran downstairs, got a gurney from a vacant ward next to N-2 and got Billy Goldsmith aboard it with no difficulty. I was glad; I was afraid we might have to fight with him and, if we did, he'd be getting cut inside. I just said, "Billy, please climb on this gurney."

"Sure, Mike," he said. "Where we going, X-ray?" That gave me a shiver. Maybe this razor blade thing was real. Once we had him on the gurney, Jerry and I tied Billy down with restraints. He didn't seem to mind. In fact, he seemed perfectly content. "Glad you believe me about the razor blades, Mike. I would never lie to my best friend."

Jerry looked at me quizzically in response to the "best friend" remark. He, no doubt, thought I might be carrying this "therapeutic community" thing a bit too far.

Racing down the corridor with the gurney, me pulling and Jerry pushing, we arrived at X-ray, where they were waiting for us. "Razor blades?" the technician laughed. "You joking?"

"I hope we are," I said.

But we weren't. The tech put the still wet X-rays up on the wall of flat lights.

"Holy shit," he said. "Never seen nothing like this." The X-rays distinctly showed eight halves of razor blades sitting in Billy's stomach. They were the clearest thing in the picture, rather pretty actually. If I was looking at that X-ray today I would think it was some kind of wacko performance art or that it had been photoshopped. But those blades were real.

The tech called in the hospital radiologist. "Holy shit," the doctor also exclaimed. Then he turned to Billy and said, "Son, how'd you get these razor blades inside your stomach."

"Ate them," Billy said matter-of-factly.

"He's from N-2," I told the doctor.

"Crazy motherfucker," the X-ray tech muttered.

The doctor nodded. "Lucky thing they haven't yet moved south. It's going to be tough enough getting them out of the stomach and dealing with any cuts there, but if they move on to his intestines, we'll have a critical situation on our hands. Okay, let's get this guy into surgery immediately." He picked up the phone, spoke to someone, and then told Jerry and me to take Billy down the corridor to surgery. "Pronto," he said, adding, "Take these X-rays with you." We raced down the corridor again with Billy. They were waiting for us in surgery. The surgeons and nurses were already putting on gowns, masks, and rubber gloves.

Before they put the anesthesia mask on Billy he said to me, "I hope you're glad I ate something, Mike."

"Yeah, Billy," I said, "very glad." I didn't know what else to say.

Jerry went back up to N-1 and I went back to N-2 to await the call that surgery was over. It was almost a relief to be back in the ward where the crazies, unlike Billy, definitely seemed crazy.

Two hours later Captain Quarter called down to N-2 and said, "Send Rockhead up here."

Quarter had received the call that Billy was out of surgery and had to be picked up. He would be kept on one of the regular medical units for a few days, and I was to be with him all the time he was there. The guys on the medical ward would handle the post-operative stuff, but someone from psychiatric was required to keep an eye on Billy. Something about regular medical wards not being responsible for patients from the psychiatric wards. "24 hours a day," Quarter said. "I can't spare anyone else from N-1 or N-2 to relieve you, so you have to handle all shifts till he's ready to come back to N-2. When they bring his food, have them bring it for you too."

"But how do I sleep?" I asked.

"That's your problem," Quarter said. "Sleep in the chair, whatever." Quarter was regular Navy, so, until then, I hadn't had much respect for him. I figured a doctor who chose the Navy as a career must be a loser. But Quarter had been dead right about Billy. If there was a loser in the present circumstances, it was me.

Jerry went with me to pick up Billy. He had been placed back on a gurney and had IVs in his arms. We had to be careful moving him with the IVs on mobile stands. There was a huge bandage on his stomach. Jerry helped me carefully off-load Billy onto a bed and then left to resume his regular duties on N-1.

But before Jerry and I took Billy down to the medical ward, the surgeon had taken me aside and asked, "You in charge of this kid?"

I told him that I was.

"Look," the surgeon continued, "this kid is severely dehydrated, suffering from malnutrition, and his blood pressure is off the charts. These needles stay in his arm and, when the bags are finished he's to be hooked up to another set. It's in his chart. Make sure the medics on the regular ward follow through. Those lazy sons of bitches don't do anything all day. See that he gets some real food into him soon. I'm putting him on a special diet: liquids for two days starting tomorrow; then more solid stuff. But no coffee or cigarettes for a week."

Whoa, I thought, obviously no razor blades, but no coffee or cigarettes for a week? It would be fun to deal with that when Billy woke up.

Which he did in a couple of hours. I was dozing in the chair by his bed when he came up out of it and groaned. The first thing he said was, "Got my cigarettes, Mike?"

"Sorry, Billy," I said. "The doctor says no cigarettes for a week."

"Then coffee. Let me have some coffee. I'm hungry."

"No coffee either, for a week. Doctors orders. Coffee has lots of acid. Your stomach couldn't take coffee just now. There's cuts in it. They have to heal."

"I'm starving," he gasped.

"These needles in your arm are feeding you. By to-morrow you'll be having soup and other soft stuff. Milk, custard. Then regular food after a couple of days. Meat and potatoes. Gonna fatten you up."

Billy looked pained. "That's not *my* regular food. Please, Mike, you can't let them do this to me. Wasn't I good? Didn't I eat my razor blades?" It was as if he was saying, *Didn't I eat my oatmeal?* "I'll starve to death," he groaned and went back under again.

I was glad he did; I didn't want to continue this conversation. In fact, I no longer wanted to have any conversation with Billy, ever, if I could help it. He was crazy, even if he hadn't seemed crazy before now. Maybe, I thought, those are the craziest ones, the ones who don't seem crazy—who betray no anxiety, who seem calm and totally rational. But then how do you distinguish between them and normal people? Maybe the crazy people are *too* normal and what makes people normal is that they're just a tad crazy. Like me.

I felt like a fool for thinking that Billy was normal, but I shouldn't have been so hard on myself. I had little experience. And even if I was a fool, I had tried to do something good. I couldn't help feeling a little disappointed, sad even. But based on the experience with Billy I vowed never to get close to a patient again, be friendly but never a friend.

Meanwhile, I was stuck by Billy's bedside. When he woke up he would want to talk. He would want his cigarettes and coffee. He would drive me out of my mind about his cigarettes and coffee.

I was determined that when I got Billy back to N-2 I would avoid him as best I could. Nothing sudden, just slowly ease off, first pretend a couple of times that I was too busy to talk. But, meanwhile, I prayed he stayed under as long as possible. I dozed a bit more in my chair.

But what about the night? Would he be up all night and want to talk? Without his gallons of coffee, maybe he would sleep. One thing was certain: with those stitches in his stomach and me sitting right there at least he wouldn't be spanking the monkey for a while. Not a lot anyway.

How I Ended Up
on the Nut Ward

⚓

Wwhile Billy slept, perhaps dreaming of razor blades and other delicacies, I thought of how I ended up working with the likes of him on a locked psychiatric ward in Japan. I wasn't even supposed to be in the Navy.

My induction took place at 39 Whitehall Street, near the southern tip of Manhattan. This was the old building Arlo Guthrie would make famous in his hilarious 1967 song "Alice's Restaurant" and in the movie based on the song. During his own induction, having once been convicted of littering, Guthrie was classified among the violent criminals of Group W and rejected for admission. In 1969 anti-Vietnam War radicals led by Sam Melville placed huge bombs in the building and blew it up.

My induction notice arrived while staying with my new wife in upstate New York, where she was attending college. I took the bus to Manhattan, arriving at Whitehall Street one cold winter day in late 1955 with a letter in my hand from the United States Army that began "Greetings."

I was sent upstairs and told to strip to my underpants or "skivvies" as they called them. Carrying my clothes in what they called a "ditty bag," I stood on long lines to be examined by a doctor, then a dentist, and finally a bald headed psychiatrist. The psychiatrist asked, "Do you like boys?"

That seemed a strange question. "Sure I like boys," I replied "why not?"

"Ever have sex with a boy?" the psychiatrist continued.

"What?!" I exclaimed. At that point in my life I'd never heard of such a thing. Young folks today learn all about homosexuality growing up, but I was so completely absorbed in figuring out girls—my new wife included—that the existence of any other kind of sexuality was unknown to me. Hey, it was the 1950s! Oral sex had yet to be "invented"—or, at least, I'd never heard of it.

The psychiatrist seemed satisfied with my responses because he told me to get dressed and go down to room D. There was only one, unmarked room downstairs, and I figured that had to be it.

Room D was a cavernous, dingy, windowless, poorly lit place painted disease green. It looked like pains had been taken to remove anything that might delight the eye. Inside, a hundred guys milled about—smoking, anxious. We must have been there fifteen-twenty minutes when a tough looking guy in army uniform with sergeant's stripes strode into the room and onto a little raised platform up front. This guy looked like he was made entirely of brass. He carried a clipboard and whacked it against his leg.

"Okay, you fucking maggots," he began, "listen up."
The response not being immediate, he said, "You fucking
deaf? I said, listen up!"

Things quieted down then. "First thing," he continued, "put out those fucking cigarettes. Nobody said you
could smoke. From now on you'll smoke only when we
fucking tell you to. You'll piss only when we fucking tell
you to and you'll shit only when we fucking tell you to.
Okay, on the double, form one straight line across the
room facing me."

We shuffled into the semblance of a line. "One
straight line, you fucking maggots. You are the sorriest
bunch of fuckers I've ever seen. Uncle Sam must be getting fucking desperate if he wants *you*. You are a bunch
of dumb, fucking fucks." I had no comprehension of what
a "fucking fuck" might be, but I had to admire this guy's
ingenuity. He could, I imagined, construct whole sen-
tences, perhaps even paragraphs, using nothing but the
"f" word.

But why did this guy have to insult us? Here we
were, beginning our service to our country, and all this
guy could do was call us names. I'm not sure what I had
been expecting, though a nice "Welcome" or "Thank you
on behalf of President Eisenhower" would have been
nice. And, yes, a stirring patriotic moment—the singing
of "The Star Spangled Banner," say. It didn't have to be a
choir. We inductees could have sung it ourselves, or they
could have just played it on a 78 rpm record. They play
the national anthem at athletic events for fans, so why
not for guys about to defend their country or whatever
it was we were about to do, it being peacetime and our
country not requiring much defense. We weren't in uniform yet, so we couldn't salute, but I did have a hankering

for "The Star Spangled Banner" and to put my hand over my heart. I'd have settled for reciting the pledge of allegiance, even with the "under God" part that had recently been added by Congress.

I wanted to feel some patriotic fervor in room D. I was a draftee, ordered into the military by my country, had my life and career and marriage interrupted. I hear the military today, all volunteer, doesn't insult recruits the way it insulted us. But in the military as I experienced it, the "f" word was *the* word applied to inductees, serving as noun, adjective, verb, and adverb and used in the present, past, future, conditional, pluperfect and any other tense. Not many years had passed since I had used the "f" word once at home and my mother stood by while I scrubbed my tongue with a bar of soap.

The sergeant continued. "Okay, you fucking maggots. This month the fucking Navy hasn't had enough enlistees. I can understand that. Who would want to be in the fucking Navy when you could be in the Army? Nothing but faggots in the Navy. I need thirty volunteers for the fucking Navy, and you've got thirty fucking seconds to make up your fucking minds."

The possibility of the Navy instead of the Army was a surprise. The Navy prided itself on never having to resort to the draft. It always had enough enlistees. I raised my hand.

"Whatya want fuckhead?'

"Sir," I asked, "isn't the Navy four years?"

"Not if you're drafted, fuckhead. Two. Same as the Army." Then he added, "Fuckhead, you better get straight with yourself. This is the military. You don't ask questions here."

Not asking questions seemed the height of stupidity. But I tried to ignore his insults because I had thirty seconds to make an important decision. It was enough. I thought of great, grey ships parting the waves, of seeing the world, of those thirteen button pants that supposedly drove women wild—though I wondered how you peed with thirteen buttons. I thought about how in the Navy there would be no dirty foxholes, no jungles, no crotch rot. Also, I had been on the swimming team in college. Water was a more natural element to me than dirt.

"Okay you fuckers time's up. Those faggots who want to be in the fucking Navy, step forward." I stepped forward immediately, "faggot" or not.

"If I point to you, give me your fucking name and go outside and get on the fucking bus. Only your last name. You're in the military now. As far as Uncle Sam is concerned, you don't have a fucking first name any more."

I was anxious: It looked like more than thirty of us had stepped forward. The sergeant began pointing at guys. "You," he said. "You. You." As he pointed and the guys gave him their names, he checked them off on his clipboard. Would I get picked? There seemed to be no logical criterion for getting picked; it was perfectly random. But finally he pointed at me, number twenty-nine, and said "You," and I was in the Navy.

Outside in the street was a grey bus with the motor running that said "United States Navy" on its side. I climbed aboard. Every seat had a box lunch on it. I sat next to a kid with a huge lantern jaw. "Where're we going?" I asked.

"How the fuck should I know," he said. This kid was catching on fast.

The bus accelerated, heading for the Holland Tunnel, and soon we were on the New Jersey Turnpike. But where were we going, somewhere in New Jersey or to California? I lurched up the aisle and approached the uniformed driver. "Sir," I said, "can you tell me where we're headed?"

"Sit the fuck down," he said. "You're fucking going where I'm fucking taking you."

"But…"

"You deaf, fuckface? This is the Navy. There are no questions here." This was the second time in fifteen minutes that I'd asked what I considered a reasonable question and been told to shut up. I would remember these two incidents when I got to boot camp, where everyone was assigned a nickname by our company commander and mine was "Questions."

Heck, I had just graduated college. That's what you did in college: ask questions. A professor of mine liked to say, "The only dumb question is the one you didn't ask." But in the Navy, or at least in my Navy, all questions were "dumb." There seemed to be a willful embrace of ignorance.

I returned to my seat. Why were these people so nasty? Well, at least "fuckface" was a new use of the "f" word—a creative addition to the language of the sergeant inside 39 Whitehall.

We continued south. I noticed signs for Delaware, then Maryland. It was almost dark when we got off the interstate and, heading down a country road, arrived at a gate with a large sign over it: U.S. NAVAL TRAINING CENTER BAINBRIDGE MARYLAND. Some tough looking, uniformed guys in white helmets that said "MP" on them, and with white clubs on their belts, opened the gate. It felt like we were going to prison. I would not pass through that gate again for eight weeks.

The bus continued past endless, dull grey buildings. Next to one of them, we piled off the bus. A guy in Navy blues, three stripes on his sleeves, stood before us. Tattoos peeked out of his sleeves.

He was holding a clipboard. The military seemed to love clipboards. "All right," he said, "muster. I call your fucking name you say 'present.' You don't say 'here.' You don't say 'yo.' You say 'present.' Nothing fucking else you fuckheads." Another friendly greeting.

The petty officer began calling out names. All of us remembered to say "present" except one fat kid who said "here."

The petty officer flew into a rage. He went up to this kid and stuck his face into his. "You are a fucking disgrace," he screamed. "You do that one more time and I will personally watch you eat your shit. For dessert you'll eat mine. I will cut off your balls and throw them onto a power line. I will tie your dick in a knot so that, for the rest of your life you can only piss sideways. Give me thirty, fuckhead."

"Thirty what, Sir?" the kid managed.

"Thirty pushups you fat fuck."

"I can't do pushups, Sir."

"Well, I'll be screwed, blued, and tattooed. You can't do pushups?! Well, I happen to know you *can* do pushups. And I know you're going to do thirty pushups right now. Lie down on the deck.

The kid complied.

"Not on your back, you fucking idiot. Dick down, ass up"

The fat kid laboriously turned over.

"You," the petty officer yelled at a muscular kid. "Show this fat fuck how to do pushups."

The muscular kid got down and started. He was told to stop after three or four.

"Okay, you fat fuck," said the petty officer. "You give me thirty. And you count out loud as you do them. Thirty. You stop at twenty-nine and you'll start all over again."

The fat kid tried to do the pushups. He could barely lower his body, and it was even harder for him to raise it. He would raise it a couple of inches, collapse, and croak out a number. Torrents of sweat ran off him. The veins of his neck were like ropes, his face beet red. I thought he might split open and die right there.

The petty officer turned to the rest of us. "Don't none of you assholes forget this fat fuck. He may not make it through boot camp but the rest of you will if you listen, never speak unless spoken to, and show that you have a pair. In eight weeks we will have turned most of you fuckheads into men."

I doubted that. From what I'd seen thus far, the challenge would be in keeping the Navy from turning us into mice. I resolved then and there to put all emotions on hold indefinitely and not let the bastards get to me. Boot camp was like a cult. And I was damned if I would drink the Kool-Aid.

The fat kid had by now finished his thirty pushups, such as they were. He was having trouble getting up. The petty officer grabbed him by the hair and yanked him onto his feet. He screamed in pain. "Shut up, fuckface," the petty officer said "unless you want to do another thirty."

He stared at his clipboard. "Which one of you is Rockland?"

Uh, oh. What was this? "Me, Sir," I said.

"Okay, you stay here. The rest of you fuckheads go in that door." Later, I would learn that whoever passed through that door got their heads shaved. Everyone looked the same after that, equally ugly, clearly what the Navy wanted. That's what boot camp proved to be about: making everyone the same, squeezing anything interesting out of you.

"Follow me," the petty officer said. "Captain Reynolds wants to see you."

I got in step behind him and we marched in the dark across a large paved area I would later learn was our drill field. They called it "the grinder." There was a light on in a low, squat building across the way. I was ushered into the building and into a room where a naval officer sat behind a metal desk. "This is him, Sir" the petty officer said.

"I'll wait outside."

"You Rockland?" the officer asked.

"Yes, Sir," I replied

"I understand you're a college graduate."

"Yes, Sir, I am," I repeated.

"You didn't do ROTC in college?"

"No, Sir."

"Well, we can remedy that. How would you like to be an officer?" He said this with a big smile, as if he was offering me the moon. "I can put you in OCS—Officers Candidate School. You'll be an officer and you'll only be obliged to do one more year of service—though, of course, we hope you'll consider a career."

"Thank you, Sir," I replied, "but I'd rather not." I felt a little bad saying this.

He was the first military person who had spoken to me as a human being. That would change.

"Why not?" Reynolds asked, incredulous.

I told him that I planned to go to graduate school after the Navy and had already been accepted. When I was drafted, the university had allowed me to put off matriculation for two years. I doubted they would allow me another year. But even if they did, I had no interest in an extra year of military service.

Reynolds became angry. "You think you're too good to be an officer in the armed forces of the United States?" he said.

"No Sir, I don't."

"Phillips," the officer called. Phillips opened the door. "Get this fuckhead out of my face." Ah, things had returned to normal: I was back to being a fuckhead. "He thinks he's too good for the Navy. Put him into boot camp with the other fuckheads he came here with."

Phillips marched me across the grinder again. On the way over he said," You are a sorry motherfucker, Rockland. Why would anyone turn down being an officer? I've been in the Navy twelve years and nobody's asked me to be an officer, and nobody will either. You must think you're hot shit."

I thought it best not to answer. Phillips was a "lifer," a guy who was going to put in his twenty years minimum in the Navy and get out with a pension. As I would learn, lifers didn't really like anyone but other lifers. They tolerated enlistees, but they really hated draftees. They hated anyone who wasn't, like them, in the military by choice.

A half hour later, my head was shaved and, in the warehouse next door, I was issued my gear. I was given steel dog tags on a chain with my name and serial number stamped on them, 488-24-63. That's a number I'll never forget. Sometimes I forget my Social Security number and have to look it up, but I'll never forget 488-24-63. Dog tags then were different from those issued in more recent years. They had grooves so they could stick them between your upper and lower teeth when you got killed. When rigor mortis set in they'd be in there solid. Or so we were told. Now, I understand, they just tie them to your big toe before sticking you in a body bag. Those dog tags around my neck were a constant reminder of my possible death while serving in the Navy. They gave me the creeps.

The two sailor hats they gave me had my last name and serial number stenciled on them too. I was also given a large canvas duffle bag—they called it a "sea bag"—and several uniforms. "Where's the thirteen button pants?" I asked the guy handing out the gear.

"Discontinued, fuckface," he said. Damn, that was one of the reasons I had chosen the Navy over the Army—those sexy pants. Also, there was a rumor they had historic meaning—stood for the original thirteen colonies. Later, I learned this was untrue but, at the time, I'd have liked that connection to history instead of plain bell bottoms with a zipper fly.

When I got to the barracks, everyone from my bus wanted to know where I had been and what had happened. "They wanted to make you an officer and you turned them down? No shit," several guys said. "You could have kicked ass, man." I tried to explain that I had no desire to kick ass, especially not in the Navy.

Jerry Simon, who would later be with me in Yokosuka, was supportive. He had gotten through half of college in Baltimore, had dropped out, and, like me, was drafted the moment he was no longer in school. "Of course you don't want to be an officer," he said. "The Navy's a crock of shit."

Still, in the ensuing weeks I sometimes wondered whether I had made a mistake not becoming an officer. Our company commander and drill instructor was that same petty officer, Phillips. He tortured us non-stop for the next eight weeks—only four hours sleep a night, marching around the grinder much of the day carrying ancient rifles, taking classes in overheated buildings where if you fell asleep Phillips would rap your head hard with his knuckles.

With little sleep, marching in the cold, and the overheated classrooms, everyone in the company was sneezing, coughing, wheezing. A few guys were sent to the base hospital, Jerry Simon one of them. "Fucking Navy," he said when I visited him. "I've got pneumonia." The Navy seemed as interested in breaking us down physically as psychologically. The point of this escaped me. It certainly didn't toughen us up. If a war had erupted just then, and our strength as warriors was required, we would have had little to contribute. Later, I would think that I didn't have to wait until I got to Yokosuka to enter a madhouse. I was in one from the moment I started boot camp.

If only the classes had been more interesting. I had thought we would learn some nautical things—how to tie knots, how to rig sails. Maybe Sea Scouts do, but to this day I can't distinguish starboard from port. Jerry said, "The only thing they're teaching us is to be dumb, to take orders and shut up. Well, fuck 'em."

"Yeah, fuck 'em," I replied. Slowly, the "f" word was becoming part of my regular vocabulary too.

The classes basically had two subjects: the Uniform Code of Military Justice—what they would do to you if you stepped out of line—and venereal disease. Movie after movie began with a sexy prostitute standing on a street corner, wriggling her hips. The rest of the movie showed the results of approaching such a person: horrible diseases. Some infected penises looked like rotten meat. Others looked like they were about to fall off. There was no mention whatsoever of the use of condoms. The movies seemed to suggest that good sailors never went near women. So what *did* they do?

The Navy seemed obsessed with venereal disease. When boot camp began we were instructed never to tuck our T-shirts into our skivvies. Phillips told us that it had to do with gonorrhea. He said, "If you have the clap and you have your T-shirt tucked in, right over your dick, when you pull your T-shirt off over your head you might get some clap in your eyes and go blind." I don't know if what he said was true, but, although I have never had gonorrhea, ever since the Navy I haven't tucked my undershirt inside my skivvies. Whenever I am in a gym locker room after working out, and see a man tuck in his undershirt, I smile. It's not so much about venereal disease; it just looks funny, like wearing socks with sandals.

One night, crossing a virtually empty mess hall after dinner, I twice felt sudden, excruciating pain. Two regular Navy guys—lifers—had kicked me in the back. I ended up on the deck ten feet away. It had apparently just been swabbed, but there had been no signs or barriers, so how was I to know? For a moment I thought I might be paralyzed for life. I moved my hands and feet and then slowly got up and staggered out of the mess hall, laughter following me.

The incident was typical of the random cruelty of the Navy. This was what those bastards considered fun.

When I got back to the barracks I talked to company commander, Phillips. I didn't expect him to be sympathetic, but there was no one else to talk to. I wanted justice. I wanted to file a complaint.

"I wouldn't do that, Questions," Phillips said.

"Why not, Sir?" I asked, several of the articles in the Universal Code of Military Justice dancing before my eyes.

"Because," said Phillips, "you don't want to end up in the brig, do you? It'll be your word against them two. And they're probably first or second class petty officers. You're a draftee seaman recruit, not worth shit. There's a better chance they'll throw you in the brig than them."

I felt like a coward, but mention of "the brig" was enough for me to drop the matter. I had seen the movie, *From Here to Eternity* two years before and remembered that Maggio, played by Frank Sinatra, had pretty well been beaten to death in the brig. Brigs weren't like jails. Marines ran them, and they beat you with clubs. Even if you didn't do anything wrong, they beat you. At least, everyone believed that.

Boot camp was enough hell without looking for more. Even the pay was an insult: $78 per month. And when you lined up to get it, a woman from the Red Cross was there, seated behind the table just past the disbursing officer with her hand out.

Giving to the Red Cross wasn't optional. Our company commander, Phillips, demanded one hundred percent participation, as if the Navy and the Red Cross were one and the same. I've had bad feelings about the Red Cross ever since. I regularly donate blood, but never through the Red Cross. Rumors were rife about Red Cross women—that they were easy lays, that they were really at Bainbridge to participate in sexual orgies. It was certainly just the fantasy of horny young men, but since I was now antagonistic to the Red Cross, there was comfort in it.

At the end of boot camp we all received orders. Mine were to attend hospital corpsmen's school for sixteen weeks right there at Bainbridge. I was glad I might learn something useful. I was also glad that Jerry had been assigned to corpsmen's school too.

There was disdain in the company for anyone going to hospital corpsmen's school. "That's for pussies, Questions," the guys in my company said. The implication was that real men went to a school where you learned how to fire the big guns on battleships or how to serve on an aircraft carrier flight crew or how to take submarines down.

Hospital corpsmen's school was a pleasure after boot camp. The abuse and the "fucking this" and "fucking that" largely stopped. They even dangled a prize in front of our class of fifty-two students. We were told that all of us, except two, would be sent to Camp Pendleton, California and attached to a Marine unit. The two with the highest grades would be sent to Japan. I vowed right then that I would be one of them. Who would want to be with the marines at Pendleton when you could go to Japan? I had never traveled overseas. This was my chance. Jerry was keen on Japan too.

He and I worked hard, studying together in the barracks. I ended up with the top score and Jerry with number two. Then our orders came through. Jerry was going to Japan. I got the same orders as everyone else in the company: Pendleton.

No way was I going to accept this. I found out who cut orders for the fifty-two of us, a warrant officer in the base personnel department. I went to see him.

At first, I got nowhere. "We go where our orders say we go," he said.

I told him I knew this, but a promise had been made and not kept.

"You some kind of wise guy?" he said. "I see here you're a college graduate. We don't do any favors for college boys."

"Sir," I replied, "I'm not asking for a favor. I'm asking to be sent where we were told the two guys with the highest scores would be sent, and the other guy got Japan."

The warrant officer told me to sit outside his office. I waited nervously. A half hour went by. I could hear him through the closed door speaking animatedly on the telephone.

Then the door opened and he said, "You are one lucky son of a bitch, Rockland. You're going to Japan." He tore up my old orders and typed new ones. "You fly to San Francisco and report to Treasure Island Navy Base. From there, you fly to Japan."

The flight to Japan ended up having three legs, the first two fraught with disaster. The MATS (Military Air Transport Service) plane from Frisco almost didn't make it into Hawaii. As we were descending, the cabin filled with smoke. One of the pilots rushed back from the cockpit and pulled out an exit window over the wing. That cleared the smoke, but now, as we continued down, a hurricane force wind tore through the cabin, paper and other debris flying along the aisles and overhead, some being sucked out into the clouds. I wondered whether anyone without his seat belt in place might have gotten sucked out too. It was terrifying.

Then we heard what sounded like a powerful explosion. Every one around me was now doubly terrified. Much later we learned what the problem had been: the landing gear wouldn't come down. The explosion was carbon dioxide canisters attached to the landing gear blowing it down, but no one from the flight deck said anything about it. Standard Navy: "We only tell you what you need to know. You're not dead, so what's your problem?"

We managed to land safely at Hickham Field, made famous during the Pearl Harbor attack in 1941. That's where the American planes were destroyed before they could get airborne. We were assigned bunks in a barracks that still had holes in it from the Japanese strafing.

This would have been an opportunity for the Navy to be creative: let us go into Honolulu, catch a swim at Waikiki Beach. Wasn't seeing the world how the Navy sold itself? But no, we were required to just sit for two days in that barracks until another plane was provided to continue our journey.

The second plane proved little better than the first. We flew through the night, crossing the International Date Line at 11 p.m. on July 13th. My birthday being July 14th, I had a one hour 21st birthday because, at 12:01 a.m. it became July 15th. A one hour 21st birthday and no one to celebrate it with but a dark plane full of snoring sailors. I wished that at least Jerry had been there, but he must have been traveling to Japan on different dates.

Lonely, I stared out the window and was aghast. One of the plane's motors was apparently not working. The prop was standing straight up, not moving.

I made my way up the dark aisle and knocked on the pilot's door. "Come in," someone called. Inside the cabin were several bunk beds with what I assumed to be pilots and navigators who were asleep. At the controls was a lone pilot. Well, he wasn't exactly *at* the controls. His hands were behind his head and his feet were atop the instrument control panel, like someone with his feet up on his desk.

"Sir," I croaked, "I have to report that one of the motors doesn't seem to be working."

"Not to worry. I've alerted Air/Sea Rescue," he replied nonchalantly.

I went back to my seat but couldn't sleep. Somebody had to stay awake. As far as I knew, there was only the pilot and me awake, and I wasn't entirely sure about him.

Around 2:00 in the morning we landed on tiny Wake Island, where two battles took place during World War II. We would remain on Wake for two days while yet another plane was requisitioned to take us on to Japan. We were assigned bunks in a Quonset hut and then made our way down to the island bar, which was also in a Quonset hut.

Sitting at the bar, I found myself engaged in conversation with a couple of sailors stationed on Wake who were blind drunk. "What do you do here?" I asked.

"Drink," one of them said, laughing.

I told them that I had just come in on a plane with one of the motors out.

"We know," they said. "We're Air/Sea Rescue." *That was comforting,* I thought.

"What kind of equipment do you have?"

"Some big row boats," was the reply.

"But if we had come down in the ocean an hour or so east of here, what would you have done?"

"Nothing," one of them said, followed up by a cackling laugh in which the other guy joined. "You would probably have been shit out of luck."

"You're kidding," I said. I looked at their faces. Drunk or not, they weren't kidding. I went back to my Quonset hut, but I didn't sleep well. And, in the morning, the Quonset was an oven. It was hot enough outside, but if you stayed in the Quonset, you cooked.

Still, I enjoyed the two days on Wake. I wandered around that sandy island, essentially just an air strip. There were these weird looking birds, "Gooney Birds," someone said. I didn't see a single palm tree, but there were collapsing Japanese bunkers and the rusting remains of small Japanese tanks along the edges of the island in the shallow water. I stepped down on the turret of one of the tanks but immediately withdrew. A giant moray eel came boiling up out of the turret heading straight for my foot.

The third leg of the trip to Japan was remarkably uneventful, considering how the first two had gone. We landed in Tokyo in the fading light of another day. A few of us were put on a bus to Yokosuka Naval Base with other guys who were already aboard.

We passed through the city of Yokosuka. Its distinct smell wafted through the bus windows: food being cooked with gobs of soy sauce. The buildings were all low and wooden and rickety, though much of the town was illuminated by neon, with loud music emanating from brightly lit bars, girls standing on every corner, and American sailors and marines walking through the town in desultory fashion, eyeing the girls and bargaining with the ones who interested them. One of the guys on the bus shouted, "Yeah, lemme at that!" Yokosuka looked like a carnival.

I found myself wishing I hadn't gotten married before coming into the Navy. I was too young. I hadn't even *begun* to sow my wild oats, and endless opportunities to do so were just outside the bus.

The base was nothing like the town: it was dark, dull, and grey. You could just make out huge warships in the harbor. MPs manned the main gate. The base, like Bainbridge, looked like a prison.

There were reminders everywhere that the base had once been in other hands. Fading Japanese writing was on some of the buildings. There were mountains at the edge of the base, I would learn, with 260 caves and 27 kilometers of deep tunnels, some with rails that would have been used for bringing up the heavy guns protected deep inside. If the rest of Japan was anything like Yokosuka, it could only have been conquered with immense American casualties.

I went to sleep in the barracks as soon as I arrived. I didn't have a room exactly, just an alcove surrounded on three sides by plywood painted grey. But an alcove was better than no separations at all, something more or less my own. It had a steel rack, a steel table, a steel chair, and a steel lamp. None too comfy, but at least I had a place to lay my books down. I would live in that alcove for most of the next year and a half.

In the morning I reported to the personnel office of the hospital, a long grey wooden building. Like the other buildings on the base it didn't have a name, just the letter "E" followed by number 22. The Navy seemed to go out of its way to depersonalize things, to insure they offered no aesthetic or intellectual pleasure. Was this to save American taxpayers money or to guarantee that everyone working in the hospital would have an unqualified commitment to mediocrity?

The hospital personnel officer was friendly enough. He was dressed in cotton whites. San Francisco being so cool, I had traveled in woolen blues, but it was summer in Japan, hot and humid, so it was clearly time to put on my own whites.

"We have an opening in Psychiatric," the personnel officer said.

"Fine," I said. Psychiatric seemed better than carrying bed pans in a regular ward, although I couldn't imagine how my sixteen weeks of medical training would apply in a psychiatric ward. I had been primarily educated in battlefield first aid—how to treat wounds, stop bleeding, the properties and dosages of drugs like morphine, how to combat shock. There had not been one word about mental illness. As far as medic's school had been concerned, there was no such thing in the Navy.

"There's N-1 and N-2, the personnel officer explained. 'N' stands for 'Neuropsychiatric,' but we just call them the 'Nut Wards.' We had another guy in from Bainbridge the other day—what's his name? Simon, I think—I put him on N-1, the open ward. The vacancy now is on N-2, the locked ward." He looked at me meaningfully.

"Fine," I repeated, "Probably more interesting than the open ward."

"That it is," he said as I walked out the door, "that it is."

Day One on "Blueberry Hill"

⚓

After changing clothes in the barracks, I walked down the long hospital corridor to N-2, the locked psychiatric ward. Maybe I could have the satisfaction of doing some good there. Maybe something about my Navy experience would prove to be worthwhile.

When I knocked on the heavy door, Jimmy Kreeg, the senior corpsman on the a.m. shift, opened it and said, "Yeah?" I couldn't see Kreeg well. He seemed to be standing in a pool of gloom.

I could hear yelling down the end of the ward. "You don't think I'm Jesus? Up yours!" someone screamed.

"I'm the new guy," I said to Kreeg.

"Yeah," he repeated without emotion. Kreeg was big and blond with thinning hair and bad skin. He'd been in the Navy fourteen years already, was a Hospital Corpsman First Class. He had three stripes; I had one. Kreeg was making a career of it—or, at least, until he had twenty years in and could get a pension and then do something else. He was a lifer but a quality guy in many ways. You couldn't say he was dedicated, but he took his work on N-2 seriously.

Kreeg held the door open just enough for me to pass through while looking over his shoulder. Patient escapes were then a major concern on N-2. "Okay, Questions, I'll show you around." I couldn't believe it. My nickname had somehow traveled to Japan with me. It must have been on my papers from Bainbridge.

Just beyond the front door, on the right, were two padded cells. Someone was in the second one peering out through the bars of the tiny window. A cigarette dangled from his twisted lips. With his pasty white skin, the guy looked like a vampire. "Hey, buddy," he said, "got a light?"

I reached into my pocket where I thought I had some matches but Kreeg grabbed my hand. "No smoking in the padded cells," he said.

"Sorry," I said, both to Kreeg and to the guy in the cell.

"Yeah, well fuck you," the guy in the cell said, sending a glob of spit my way that whizzed by my ear, hit the wall behind me, and slowly dribbled down. I'd been on N-2 only one minute and someone already hated me.

"Who's that?" I asked Kreeg as we moved further into the ward.

"Stratomeyer. Raped and strangled some little Japanese girl. The shrinks are ready to testify at his trial. Marines are taking him back to the brig today so we put him in the cell. Crazy bastard is dangerous; has nothing to lose."

Stratomeyer at the front of the ward and some Jesus guy at the back were enough, but, in-between, the patients were crammed in tight and they were all checking me out, estimating how much shit I would take. I instantly knew I didn't want to be in N-2. It was the setting for a horror movie.

There was a raised platform up front with a desk for the medics. The patients' racks ran down the right side of the ward. The more serious patients generally occupied the lower racks, the catatonics especially so that they were more easily accessible for us to feed, clean, and dress. On the left side of the ward were two small offices for the psychiatrists. They were dark, grim places, with no windows. The shrinks rarely used them, except to go one on one with newly admitted patients to determine whether they were ready to move immediately to the open ward. They also met in there to scope out the murderers. When they did they alerted the medics and kept the door open. With some of the murderers they even asked one of us to be in the room with them in case some muscle was necessary to restrain a patient. A straightjacket hung on the back of each door.

Commander Robinson, the number two shrink after Quarter, was a little, finicky guy who only came down to N-2 if he absolutely had to and, even then, he always acted like he couldn't care less. A Freudian, he was interested in neurotics, not psychotics. Nurse Kelly only came on the ward to hand out medications, but this didn't scotch the talk among the patients that she, like Red Cross women, was sex crazed. Quarter came down at least once a day because he was responsible for both wards, but, like Robinson, he passed the better part of his days in the more pleasant and brighter offices upstairs on the open ward. Most of the time we medical corpsmen were on our own on the locked ward.

Lieutenant Robby Johnston, a pudgy, young psychologist from Indiana, was the only one who put in regular hours in the shrinks' offices on N-2. He had an open door policy: anyone could see him at any time, patients or staff. But he had few takers. Everyone looked at him as a naive goody-two-shoes; he had been nicknamed "the missionary."

Robinson clearly didn't care about N-2, Quarter cared about it only because he had to, and Johnston may have cared about it too much.

Just past the shrinks' offices was a large head with urinals, toilets and showers. There were no stalls or doors in the head. You shit and showered openly. Kreeg told me that one patient had tried to strangle another in there months before and Quarter had brought in a Japanese carpenter to remove the stalls.

At the back of the ward was a circle of steel folding chairs. "Johnston runs the group therapy session here at ten o'clock every morning," Kreeg explained. "You just missed today's."

Beyond the chairs was the back door. Kreeg opened it with a key and ushered me out into the yard. It had a basketball court, the rims rusty, no nets. "You play basketball?" Kreeg asked.

"J. V. in high school," I said. "Decent jump shot."

"Good," Kreeg said. "When you play with the patients run 'em ragged. Full court press all the way. Exercise keeps 'em calm. Better than the drugs."

Kreeg may not have been an intellectual, but he seemed level headed and fair. On N-2, he had the responsibility but not the authority. In the military there are the officers and there are the men. Period. It's feudal. You could be a hero and they still wouldn't make you an officer. What a college degree had to do with being a good officer was beyond me.

Kreeg, as the ranking petty officer on N-2, made the assignments for all three shifts. He decided when we moved from a.m. to p.m. to night shift. Generally, you did about two months on a shift and then moved to another. Each time you had to relearn how and when to sleep.

We went back inside. Kreeg locked the back door and took me into one of the shrinks' offices, unlocking a steel file drawer. He took out a set of keys and showed me how to attach them to my pants. "When your shift is over," he said, "you give the keys to your replacement. You don't put them down. You don't just hand them to him. You wait till he's got them hooked on before you leave."

"Roger that," I said. While just about everything in the Navy was unattractive to me, I rather liked saying "Roger that," which means heard and understood. Sometimes, all these years later, I still say it.

The lunch cart came on the ward pushed by a burly guy everyone called "Chef."

Most of the patients got up and helped themselves. I heard one of the patients grumble something about saltpeter in the food.

"Yeah," another said. "That's how they keep our peckers down. Not that I mind. If they didn't give us all that saltpeter the faggots would be on somebody in a jiff. Also," he continued, "with no pussy available I'd rather not be wanting any."

Saltpeter in the food was a universally subscribed to myth in the Navy: food laced with it to dampen sexual desire—especially in boot camp and aboard ship and in confined places like locked psychiatric wards. To this day I have no idea if it was true. But to play it safe I never ate anything on the ward except an occasional candy bar.

"Why don't you get started feeding one of the cats?" Kreeg said. We didn't want them to hear us say "catatonics," so we said "cats." Not that it would have made any difference: they didn't seem to listen to anything you said anyway. I went to the lunch cart, filled the compartments of the all purpose steel tray and took it over to one of the guys who was seated on his rack staring into space. I pulled up a chair.

Feeding him wasn't easy. Only by pressing the spoon or fork against his lips would he open them, and even then half the food dribbled down his chin and landed in his lap and, if I wasn't careful, in mine. It was like feeding an infant, but especially frustrating with the cats because they were grown men. You had to keep telling yourself these guys weren't doing this just to piss you off.

After lunch I made a point of going around the ward and introducing myself to the patients. In the case of the catatonics I had to grab a hand and shake it, with no response, not even a meeting of eyes. It was like tugging on a rope. One patient, a suicide, thought it was weird that I was introducing myself. "What the fuck for?" he said when I offered him my hand. "They tell me you're from New York. Well, this ain't Park Avenue."

I told him I was from the Bronx, grew up in a tenement.

"Yeah," he said, "well the way I see it all of New York is Park Avenue." And, he added, "You're here eight hours, I'm here twenty-four. You do twenty-four sometime and then we might have something to shake hands about."

I met Randy Townsend and Walter Barker, the other two staff members on the a.m. shift with Kreeg and me. The three of them were the guys I almost always served shifts with throughout my year-and-a-half in Japan, so we were a team of sorts and got to know each other well. Townsend was a high school dropout. He was tall and skinny, quirky, the joker among us but with a mean streak. When I asked him where he was from he said, "Nobody's business," but I soon learned he had grown up in some hollow in West Virginia where all the other men in his family were coal miners. The Navy had been his escape from all that dirt and danger. "And look where it got me," he said, "to the dirtiest, most dangerous place of all."

I felt drawn to Barker, especially when he extended his hand, said "Welcome to the nut ward," and asked me to call him "Wally." Townsend would always be "Townsend." I would keep my distance from him. As for Kreeg, I would always call him "Kreeg" because he was the senior guy and, though nice enough, didn't invite familiarity.

Townsend had tattoos on both arms, which turned me off to him. Tattoos weren't hip then the way they are today; they were low class. I never knew a draftee with a tattoo, nor any of the officers. I only saw them on lifers and enlistees and, when I saw them, I thought, "Bunch of losers!"

One of Townsend's tattoos was an anchor—"just like Popeye's," he would say—and the other had a heart with the name "Ginger" inscribed inside it. I asked him who Ginger was and he frowned and said, "I don't want to talk about that." I gathered that Ginger had proven a temporary amour, but now Townsend was stuck with her for life.

Wally Barker was a short, chubby black kid. Standing next to Townsend the two looked like a mixed race Mutt and Jeff. Wally was from Flint, Michigan. He couldn't get a job in the auto industry so he'd joined the Navy—but not before finishing one year of junior college.

Wally and Townsend already seemed to know something about me. They were enlistees, so I was the only draftee among the four of us and, as a result, somewhat suspect—especially as far as Townsend was concerned. Being a college graduate from New York didn't help in my relationship with him either. "You're not going to lay any intellectual shit on me, are you?" he asked. "You're not going to tell me to read Shakespeare, are you, Questions?" There it was again. Townsend knew my nickname too. Well, I thought, if I was "Questions" then I was "Questions." There were worse things to be.

Townsend said he'd never met a Jew before. "They told me in church back home that you Jews got horns," he said. When he said "Jews," it sounded like "Chews." "Where's your horns, man?"

"Sorry to let you down on that," I said. "They sawed them off in boot camp when they shaved my head. My sailor hat wouldn't fit over them."

"No shit," Townsend said. For more than a moment, I think he believed me.

I decided to give as good as I got. "But Townsend," I said, "where's your red neck?" Townsend didn't find that funny. In fact, as I would learn, he never found anything funny unless he said it.

Still, he was a member of the team I worked shifts with. On a.m. we were all together; on p.m., three of us; on night shift two. On a locked psychiatric ward it's as if you're in a bunker with the other staff and you're surrounded by the patients, many of whom are dangerous. I always felt Barker and Kreeg had my back and I had theirs, but Townsend was a different matter. If I were ever in a jam I could imagine Townsend saying "tough shit" and walking away.

While Townsend and I were talking we heard yelling from the front of the ward. Smoke was billowing out of Stratomeyer's cell. We ran. Kreeg and Wally were already there peering into the cell. Someone had apparently given Stratomeyer matches. He had torn padding off the walls and set it on fire at the back of the cell. He sat on the floor in the middle laughing maniacally. "You sonsabitches fuck with me, I fuck with you," he shouted.

"We'd better get him out of there," Wally said.

"Nah," Kreeg said. "Let him cook a while. Teach him a lesson." Townsend laughed, he was enjoying this, but Wally looked anxious, and I sure was. I kept thinking the whole hospital was made out of wood. It was a firetrap, especially our ward. The patients were locked in, and we were locked in with them.

Kreeg calmly got a straightjacket from one of the shrinks' offices. He took a fire extinguisher down from the wall by the front door and handed it to me. By this time the cell was full of smoke and Stratomeyer was coughing. "You sonsabitches gonna get me out of here?" he yelled through the smoke. I could hardly see him.

"Okay," Kreeg said, "now!" He opened the cell door and he, Townsend, and Barker jumped through the smoke and fell upon Stratomeyer, who tried to kick them. I went to the back of the cell and put out the fire, the foam stuck to the padding. I had never used a fire extinguisher before; it was fun—all that power. The other guys muscled Stratomeyer into the straightjacket, carried him out of the cell, and dumped him onto his rack.

But he wouldn't lie still. He kept rolling from side to side, cursing and spitting. Some of the other patients drifted over to talk to him. There would always be a certain patient solidarity on N-2, them against us.

Not long after, two marines arrived. While they stood by, we removed Stratomeyer's straightjacket, but he quickly rolled out the other side of the rack and ran down to the far end of the ward. The marines ran after him, clubs in hand. Stratomeyer grabbed chairs from the group therapy session circle and heaved one after another at the marines, yelling, "Stay away from me, mother fuckers." The marines each folded a chair to use as a shield and slowly closed in on him, banging with their clubs on the chairs they were holding. It was a frightening sound, barbaric, like some wild native rite, but it didn't seem to faze Stratomeyer. Then, just as he was lifting another chair to throw at one of the marines, the other rushed in and clubbed him across the shoulders with a sickening thunk. He hit him so hard the club seemed to bend and bury itself in his flesh. Stratomeyer dropped like a rock.

The marines got him into handcuffs and shackles and stood him up. He was groggy.

"March," they said, and Stratomeyer shuffled towards the front of the ward, a marine on each side of him. He looked like he was being taken off to his execution; you could almost hear the drum rolls. The other patients silently parted to let the detail pass by. "Take it easy, Strat," one of the patients said in a quiet voice. "Get some pussy for us," another called. The Jesus guy raised his hand in blessing and said, "Go in peace, my son." Despite his being a crazy murderer, even I felt some sympathy for Stratomeyer.

I never did learn what happened to him after he was taken out of our ward. In fact, I rarely heard what happened to any of our patients once they left N-2. New patients always took their place, accompanied by new problems and dangers.

That first day a longtime patient on the ward severely bit my arm. I should have been warned about him by Kreeg, but he hadn't yet had much of a chance to orient me. This guy had a little 45 rpm record of Fats Domino's great 1956 rendition of "Blueberry Hill" and played it nonstop on the little phonograph he cradled in his arms like a baby. As I would find out later, the other medics in the hospital kept hearing the song coming through our windows and had dubbed our ward with the nickname "Blueberry Hill." "Oh," they would say snickering, "so you work on Blueberry Hill?" Even after this guy was air evacuated back to the States our ward kept the nickname. Like "Questions," nicknames stuck.

I loved the song "Blueberry Hill," but not after hearing it all day long. And the words seemed to mock the situation the patients and everyone working on the ward were in.

I found my thrill
On Blueberry Hill

If I was sure of anything, it was that no one was going to find his thrill on *our* Blueberry Hill.

Every time the song ended there'd be the scratching, the guy would lift the needle, and he'd start it over again. "You're driving me nuts," a patient screamed at him.

I thought I had an obligation to intercede. I didn't know his name—everyone simply called him "Blueberry Hill"—but I went up to him and said, "How about you give the song a rest a while?"

He didn't answer, just stared at me with a look of pure hatred.

"Maybe you'll let me hold the record for a while," I said, reaching out my hand. Big mistake. Quicker than a rattlesnake he struck, sinking his teeth into my forearm. I came very close to punching him with my other hand, but I already knew you didn't hit patients, no matter what. I was bleeding all over the floor. Kreeg sent me down to the emergency room where I got six stitches and a tetanus shot.

"What about rabies?" I asked the doctor. I didn't want rabies shots. I'd had them as a kid when a dog bit me, so I knew they gave you fourteen shots then, one a day, clockwise around your belly button. I remember the needle as being so long it looked like it would come out the other side of you. The shots burned and raised huge welts.

I was relieved when the doctor said, "You've got him quarantined on your ward. Just keep an eye on him. If he starts acting crazy…"

"He *is* crazy," I quickly said.

"Yeah," the doctor said, "but I mean something new, flips out altogether. And if he starts foaming at the mouth."

This guy was on our ward not just for murder but for cannibalism; his chart said he had eaten chunks of his Japanese girlfriend after killing her. And he had all but taken a chunk out of me.

The Stratomeyer and Blueberry Hill guy incidents made me think my first day on the ward was exceptional, but I would soon learn that it wasn't. Almost every day things happened that I had never experienced before. N-2 was on another planet; it was an alternate reality.

And, looking back, I feel some affection for the whole horrible experience. Maybe it's because N-2 was something that was so bad, it was good. Well, not really good, but strong, like a bad smell you get used to and may even come to like. It certainly made a lasting impression on me. I never had any nightmares while working on N-2—maybe because every day, every eight hour shift I put in on that ward, was nightmare enough.

Outside of N-2 there was a busy military base and, beyond that, all of Japan. But N-2 had a reality all its own.

For all I know the Navy, the real Navy—destroyers, submarines, aircraft carriers—is a fine, proud, and useful institution. Without it, certainly during the World War II period, the forces of evil would likely have taken over the world. Maybe those television commercials they have these days to get people to join the Navy have some truth to them. They always show an aircraft carrier and say, "America's Navy: A global force for good." But my feelings about the Navy, then and now, are conditioned by the fact that most of the people I knew in it were crazy. The Navy I experienced seemed to be a global force for insanity.

I can't say that my military service wasn't interesting. It certainly was that. Just because you dislike something doesn't mean it can't be interesting—looking back on it anyway. It kinda reminds me of what Charles Dickens wrote about shaky wooden railroad trestles in his 1842 book *American Notes* after he visited our country. "They are amazing contrivances once passed."

The Navy Way

⚓

The second day was just as eventful as the first. Shortly after I arrived on the ward for the a.m. shift, 7:00 a.m.–3:00 p.m., my right arm bandaged, a Japanese tailor showed up to repair Stratomeyer's ravages of the second padded cell. "You lock, yes?" he said to me. "I no want crazy people come in here." I wasn't sure what to do, so I told Kreeg and he locked the cell door. "Me get out later, yes?" the tailor said, a worried look on his face. He seemed not entirely certain we would let him out when he had finished his work.

The Americans were as strange and unpredictable to him as he was to us. We thought the Japanese all looked alike and they thought we all looked alike, the black and Asian guys included. We thought the Japanese were inscrutable and I suspect they thought we were too. The war had ended only eleven years before. What if we Americans still harbored resentments? What if we kept the tailor locked up in the padded cell for a while just for fun?

"Not to worry, Papasan," Kreeg said. That was about the only Japanese most sailors knew, "papasan" and "mamasan," and it wasn't even Japanese. Well, the "san" part was—a term of respect added to names. But except for going into Yokosuka town and getting laid once in a while the guys who worked in the hospital could have been in Iowa for all that they were experiencing Japan. Japan was, for them, some kind of joke, a place where people were so backward they ate with sticks. They talked about "the round eyes" (us) and "the slant eyes" (them). Deep inside they thought the Japanese were ignorant because they couldn't speak English. Townsend would say, "You know what? They lost the war. Fuck 'em. Let 'em learn English."

We had already shaved half the patients when the food cart came on the ward with breakfast and Kreeg said, "Why don't you work on the three catatonics, Questions. See if you can get the cats fed and washed up by group time." I wondered what catatonics could contribute to group therapy and whether they got anything out of it. I figured they never said anything and just stared straight ahead, which proved to be true.

The cats were slow work. The other patients bolted down their breakfasts, half of them got shaved, and Townsend took some of them outside to play basketball. Wally played monopoly with another group. I'd have much rather been doing what Townsend or Wally were doing, but, as the new guy, I needed to prove myself, so I didn't say anything.

One of the catatonics had totally shit himself and his bed. The smell was terrible, and dealing with the guy's pajamas and bedding was awful. I gagged several times. I used a spatula to scrape the shit off into a toilet bowl and then put the bedding and pajamas into the bottom of the laundry cart that came on the ward each morning. Clean linen and pajamas were on top, soiled went below. Then I steered the catatonic down to the head and got him showered, not easy to do without getting myself dirty and wet too.

It took me till almost 10:00 to finish the catatonics. Then, one by one, I led them to the back of the ward and got them seated for the group therapy session. The other patients filled in around them.

Robby Johnston, the psychologist, ran the group therapy meetings on the open ward at eight-thirty and on the locked ward at ten. "Okay," he said, "who has something to report?"

Silence.

Johnston was determined to get a conversation going. "I heard there was a fire on the ward yesterday," he said.

The silence continued. Johnston looked unhappy. "Well," he said, "you don't have to discuss the fire, but how did you feel about it?" Johnston was big into how you *felt* about something. It seemed to interest him more than the thing itself. But the silence continued.

I understood it. What could be anything but obvious about feelings concerning a fire in a padded cell on a locked psychiatric ward?

"This is a therapeutic community," Johnston said. "We help each other by talking about our problems and commenting on the problems of others." Then, seeking to ingratiate himself with the patients, Johnston said, "We all have problems. Even I have problems."

"Yeah," one of the suicides with wrapped hands said. "You're a pussy." General laughter greeted this remark, and I tried to keep a straight face. If I'm not mistaken, even one of the catatonics seemed to faintly smile, making me think he might not be as out of it as I had thought.

I could see that one advantage of being on a psychiatric ward as a patient is that you could say anything you wanted to, or about, an officer and there would be no repercussions. You were a walking "insanity plea."

Johnston did seem somewhat effeminate or, at least, more effeminate than the four gay guys on the ward, three of whom didn't seem effeminate at all. Pussy or not, Johnston seemed happy that he had gotten one of the patients to say something. "I feel comfortable with my masculinity so you're welcome to think or say anything you want about me," Johnston said to the suicide, "but why do you feel so uncomfortable with yours that you have to call me a name?"

"I don't feel uncomfortable with my masculinity," the suicide said.

"Then why did you try to kill yourself?" Johnston asked.

"That's none of your fucking business," the patient said.

"Oh, but it is," Johnson retorted. "It's the business of all of us. There's no way you can be helped unless you're honest with everyone here about why you tried to kill yourself."

Before the suicide could respond, the session was brought to a halt when Kreeg, who had been looking about, said, "Where's Clark?" I didn't know who Clark was, but Townsend and Wally did, and so did Johnston. "Probably in the head," Wally said.

Kreeg looked quickly into the head and shouted, "Not here."

Johnston took charge. "I want everyone to help on this, patients too. Fan out throughout the ward. Look under every rack and under the covers. Check outside in the rec yard, Kreeg. Check the padded cells. And let's all meet back here in one minute." The ward was so small a minute would be sufficient.

Everyone but the catatonics got up and began scouring the ward to look for Clark, some of the patients gleeful, as if they were on a treasure hunt. But Clark was nowhere on the ward. "The fucker must have escaped," Townsend said.

Just then the ward phone rang on the front desk. "Get that, Questions," Kreeg said to me.

I ran to the front desk. A voice said, "I'm calling from the laundry. I think we have one of yours here. He came out in the laundry cart. Smells like shit."

I told Kreeg. "Damn," he said, "I'm going to have to report this." He told Wally and me to get Clark.

When we got back with Clark, a little kid who could have easily fit inside the bottom of the laundry cart, we learned that a staff meeting had been called for 3:00, when the p.m. crew would be coming on duty and we would not yet have left.

We met at the back of the ward, seated in the same chairs used for the group therapy session. Captain Quarter, his white mustache bristling, presided, and Robby Johnston, Miriam Kelly, the nurse, and the other shrink, Commander Robinson, were all in attendance, along with we four a.m. corpsmen and the three p.m. ones.

After the preliminaries, during which everyone was briefed on the incident, Quarter said, "This is the third escape from this ward. The admiral made it clear to me last time: 'If someone escapes from N-2 again, the responsible party will appear before me for disciplinary action.'"

"Kreeg," Quarter continued, "two of the three escapes have taken place during the current a.m. shift. I'm holding the a.m. shift responsible. Decide who's responsible, either all four of you or one of you. By 07:00 tomorrow I want the name, rank, and serial number of the person or persons responsible on my desk."

As we went off duty, Kreeg said to Wally, Townsend, and me, "Let's go down by the harbor and talk about this."

We sat on the rocks, looking out at the massive grey warships in front of us. Kreeg said, "Okay, somebody's got to take the rap for this. Which of you had anything to do with the bottom of the laundry cart?"

"Well, I did," I said. "I put that cat's shitty pajamas and sheets in there."

"Anybody else have anything to do with the bottom of the laundry cart?" Townsend and Wally said nothing.

"Okay," Kreeg said, "You'll have to take the rap, Questions."

"What?!" I couldn't believe it. My second day on the job and I wasn't even in Japan when the other two escapes took place. I hadn't wheeled the cart off the ward, a guy from laundry had. "Clark wasn't in the cart when I put the shitty laundry in there," I argued.

"I know," Kreeg said, but you're the only one who can be connected to the laundry cart."

"Jeezus," I said, "I just got here."

"That's why the admiral will go easy on you. Tell him you just didn't know any better. If it was me or Townsend or Barker he'd throw the book at us. You'll see: it won't be a big deal."

"This isn't fair," I said.

"I know," Kreeg said, "but the boys and I will appreciate your taking the rap. Someone has to. Either you take it or we'll all have to. You heard Captain Quarter."

"This is wrong," I said.

"This is the Navy," Kreeg said. "There's the right way, the wrong way, and the Navy way."

I would hear that line often: "the right way, the wrong way, and the Navy way."

"Also," Kreeg continued, "guys who have been here a while deserve a break. It's traditional: new guys take the rap. That's the Navy way too. Think of it as part of your initiation."

"My initiation into what?" I continued to argue. "My initiation into how the Navy way and the wrong way are the same?"

"Whatever," Kreeg said.

Townsend was nodding in approval of what Kreeg had said. "Yeah," he said authoritatively, "That's the Navy way." Wally didn't say anything. It was clear: either I took the rap or I would have to live with the disdain, if not the wrath, of my colleagues every minute of every day.

I was in a damned if you do, damned if you don't. But if all four of us would have to take the rap otherwise, maybe my taking it would be no worse for me. And I had to have these three guys on my side working on N-2.

Okay, I would go see the admiral. But I didn't want the other guys thinking I was a sucker; I just didn't say anything. I thought back to boot camp and all that lecturing about the Uniform Code of Military Justice. Justice? Yeah, sure. Someone had to be hung, and I was elected.

The next day, an hour after I arrived on N-2, there was a phone call from Captain Quarter. I was to see him in his office on the open ward immediately.

Without a word, he handed me a piece of paper. It read:

CAPTAIN'S MAST
HOSPITALMAN 3rd CLASS MICHAEL ROCKLAND
TO APPEAR BEFORE ADMIRAL WILLIAM HINKLEY
17:00 HOURS

Jeez, I thought. A Captain's Mast. I had no idea what that was, but it sounded awful. Did they tie you to a mast and whip you with a cat-o'-nine-tails? Was it a court martial? Was I going to the brig? Would the marines soon be coming for me with their clubs the way they came for Stratomeyer?

The rest of the day I did my job but I had nothing to say to Kreeg, Townsend, and Wally. When we went off duty at 3:00 p.m. Kreeg said, "I hope there's no hard feelings." I didn't answer. Wally said, "Best of luck." Townsend said, "Hang in there, motherfucker." I didn't respond to them either.

I went back to the barracks to freshen up and change clothes. Then I went looking for the admiral's office, which was tucked away in a far corner of the base down by the ships.

I got there at ten minutes to five. It wasn't till almost six that I was ushered in by his aide who had earlier told me, "When you enter the admiral's office don't just walk: march up to a point about ten feet from his desk and stand at attention. Don't say anything. Whatever you do don't ask him any questions. I hear that's your nickname, 'Questions.'" How had my nickname traveled to the base commander's office? Kreeg? Quarter? "So don't be a wise guy: just respond to what the admiral says and it'll go better for you. Understood?"

I nodded.

"Are you Hospitalman 3rd class Rockland?" the admiral asked.

"Yes, sir"

"Do I understand you take full responsibility for the escape yesterday of a patient, one William Clark, from the locked neuropsychiatric ward, N-2?

"Yes, Sir," I said, "but I believe there is a special circumstance."

"And what is that?"

"Yesterday was my second day on the job."

"But you take full responsibility?"

"Yes, Sir." What else could I do? The Navy had its own Law of Omerta. It could teach the mafia a thing or two.

"Rockland, why is your arm bandaged?"

"A patient bit me two days ago, Sir."

"The one who escaped."

"No, Sir. Another patient."

"On your first day?"

"Yes, Sir."

"Stitches?"

"Six, Sir."

"Okay, then. You're new and you're injured. I'm giving you a light sentence: two weeks confinement to base. You go to work and you can go anywhere on base after work, but you may not have liberty off the base for the next two weeks."

"Thank you, Sir," I said.

"And Rockland," he added, "Something like this happens again—the sentence will be severe."

"Yes, Sir," I said. "Thank you, Sir."

"Dismissed," the admiral said.

I did an about face and marched out of the admiral's office thinking, "Not so bad." I had been afraid I would be sent to the brig and, instead, I just couldn't go off base for two weeks. No big deal. At least in this instance the Navy way, however wrong and unjust, had proven tolerable.

Back at the barracks Kreeg, Barker, and Townsend were waiting for me. "Whatja get?" Kreeg asked.

"Two weeks confinement to the base."

Townsend whistled. Wally said, "Way to go, man."

Kreeg said, "Great news." He put his arm around my shoulder. "Let's go over to the club and get drunk. I can get you guys in as my guests. Rock, your drinks are on me."

I was glad he was now calling me "Rock," not "Questions." In fact, from that point on, none of the crew called me "Questions." They either called me "Mike" or "Rock." Wally made it even better: he sometimes referred to me as "The Rock." That felt good.

"And," Kreeg continued, "when your two weeks are up we'll all go into Yokosuka and celebrate in style. I know a great place, The House of Ten Thousand Flowers. Two bucks instead of one, but clean, beautiful girls. We need to get you laid, boy."

Whatever they thought before, the guys fully accepted me now. I had taken shit and not whined, complained, or squealed. The Navy and its ways were as crazy as the patients on our ward, but I was a "regular" now; I had been admitted to the club. We all got drunk that night and staggered back to the barracks, our arms around each other, singing. Kreeg was a surprisingly good tenor.

But when the two weeks were up I didn't want to go into Yokosuka with the guys. I told them I was married.

At first they didn't believe me. "You ain't married," Townsend said. "You're just a kid."

"True," I said, "but I *am* married."

"So what?" Kreeg said. "I'm married too. She's stateside. What she doesn't know ain't hurting her. Where's your wife?"

"State-side," I replied.

"So what the fuck, man?" Townsend said.

Wally didn't say anything, just nodded.

I'll admit it: I was sorely tempted. Yokosuka was one big candy store of women, costing virtually nothing. And The House of Ten Thousand Flowers sounded particularly enticing. Part of me—to be honest a large part of me—really wanted to go there with the guys.

"My wife's probably coming over here in a few months," I said.

"No shit," Townsend said.

"Would I shit you about something like that?" I said, angrily. I really wanted to go with the guys but wouldn't, so I didn't want to talk about it anymore.

Kreeg said, "Why don't you come with us and just have a drink at the bar? They've got great drinks there with pretty little paper umbrellas in them that open and close. You can give them to your wife when she comes. Relax. You'll stay in the bar while we go upstairs."

"Okay," I said. I'd never been to a whore house. I told myself I could write about it some day.

So I went with them. The House of Ten Thousand Flowers was at the end of a side street and was beautiful in the night with its colored paper lanterns and path of polished stones surrounded by a garden of boulders and a little brook running under a small wooden bridge. Not just women, but Feng Shui. After each guy had picked out someone, I sat in the bar, with beautiful Japanese women milling about me in kimonos, shushing across the woven rice stalk tatami floors in their slippers, tee-heeing and shyly covering their mouths with their fingers when they laughed.

One of the prettiest women came over to me and said, "Maybe we take bath together *with happy ending.*" She moved her clenched fist up and down in a slow, graceful motion. "You like?"

"I like," I responded. "But not today."

"You come back some day. You ask for Yoko."

I assured her I would just to end the conversation.

I knew that I'd feel better about myself for not having anything to lie to my wife about. It was pleasant enough just sitting there with a mysterious red drink in my hand, looking at the women, fingering the little umbrella, and then getting more drinks and more umbrellas.

Pleasantly drunk, I found myself reconciled to things. There would even come a time when, much as I hate to admit it, the Navy Way would work in my favor. But when I awakened the morning after going to the House of the Ten Thousand Flowers, no longer drunk, my first thoughts were, *Fuck the Navy* and *Fuck the Navy Way.*

The Two Jesuses

⚓

T he patient who thought he was Jesus fell into the category we medics called "looneys" or "whackjobs." The Navy didn't let him grow a beard while on active duty, but on our ward nobody insisted he be shaved (we worried enough about razor blades after the Billy Goldsmith incident, so if a patient didn't want to shave that was just fine). Though this Jesus guy's beard wasn't long, he tried to tease it into some kind of elongated, curly shape, using rubber bands. He would walk around all day with these red rubber bands on his face. To affect biblical robes, he wore his bathrobe all the time, even though it was very hot in Japan in those pre-air conditioned summer days, and when we opened the windows, reaching through the steel cages that surrounded them to raise the sashes, the air outside was even hotter. To compensate, our Jesus often didn't wear pajamas under his robe.

No one cared particularly until the day he was walking around and Nurse Kelly—the only women in the U.S. Navy I knew in Japan were nurses—came on the ward to distribute medications just when Jesus's bathrobe parted and his business was hanging out. One of the patients said, "Damn, would you look at the schlong on that Jesus dude?" Another said, "You can't be Jesus. Jesus was Jewish, so he was circumcised. You ain't circumcised, so you ain't no Jesus."

"Jesus was not circumcised," he retorted; "he was Christian. Only Jews cut off the ends of their dicks."

This Jesus guy could really get belligerent, especially when it came to politics. He believed the United States government had been taken over by aliens from another planet. "Godless communists all of them," he would say, "faggots too." He warned anyone who would listen that these communist faggot aliens were trying to change the United States Constitution. "And we can't let them do it because of who wrote the Constitution."

"Who?" someone would ask.

"Me. I wrote the Constitution."

"What about the amendments? Who wrote them?"

"I wrote them too," he would say. "Those communist faggot aliens always fight me on the second one, trying to take away our guns. Well, I say bullshit to that. We need guns or those communist faggot aliens will take over the country."

Our Jesus would keenly display the "stigmata" on the palms of his hands. As best we could tell, these were sores he had given himself by vigorously scratching his palms with his long brown finger nails, nicotine stained because he smoked nonstop. Each time the sores on his hands began to heal, he would scratch them again till they bled.

The "stigmata" caused religious controversy on the ward. One patient said, "Jesus was nailed to the cross. Those sores are just on your palms. They don't come through to the other side. If they don't come through to the other side you couldn't have been nailed." Our Jesus didn't respond to this criticism but soon was spotted working away on the other side of his hands too, rubbing them on the pointy steel edge of his rack. We medics kept an eye on him to insure he didn't sever a vein. He was skinny and his veins stuck out. As it was, he developed an infection on one of his hands and had to be treated with penicillin and bandaged. The bandage on one hand rather put a crimp in his stigmata efforts.

Our Jesus had sad brown eyes, so he did look a little like Jesus—assuming anyone actually knows what Jesus looked like. He took great offense whenever anyone questioned his legitimacy. He'd say things like, "Go and sin no more." But that was mild. Usually, he would say things to unbelievers like, "Kiss my holy ass, you heretic motherfucker. Getting burned at the stake would be too good for you. I'm going to talk to my father about you. He and I are going to really fuck you up."

I couldn't resist getting into conversation with the Jesus guy. "How do you know God's male and not female?" I asked him.

"It says it right in the Bible. It says God is a he."

"Yeah," I said, thinking I had him trapped, "but that's because men wrote the Bible. If women had written it, God would have been a she."

"Bullshit," he said. "Neither men nor women wrote the Bible. God wrote it—with a little help from me, on the new part, of course—and he damn well knew whether he was a he or a she. And I damn well know whether he's my father or my mother."

I decided after that to stay out of theological discussions with our Jesus. I didn't want him claiming he was being religiously persecuted, leastwise by me, not being Christian.

The name of the Jesus guy on our ward was Smith, but you had to call him "Jesus" or he didn't respond. During the day he didn't cause much trouble, but at night, in his sleep, he would moan "Jesus, Jesus, Jesus." This was confusing: if he was calling to Jesus, how could he *be* Jesus? "Maybe that's how he rehearses," Wally said.

One patient opined, "Maybe he thinks he's Jesus when he's awake, but in his sleep he calls to Jesus because he isn't Jesus but his soul belongs to Jesus."

"Oh, yeah?" answered another patient. "His soul may belong to Jesus but, if he doesn't cut this shit out, his ass is mine. He wakes me up one more time, I kick the shit out of him. I would crucify the bastard, but we got no nails and boards. Maybe we hang him up on his rack. It would make everyone happy, him most."

Smith woke up half the ward with his moaning. Other patients would yell, "I don't care if you're Jesus, Moses, or Mohammed. Shut the fuck up."

One of the medics then on night crew said, "This 'Jesus, Jesus, Jesus' thing gives me the creeps. The ward's stone black, everyone's snoring, and then you start to hear this guy moaning 'Jesus' over and over. I keep thinking some zombie is crawling towards me between the racks and is gonna eat my brain."

One day, during the morning group therapy session, Lieutenant Johnston was able to coax some patients into voicing their feelings about our Jesus. One patient said, "This son of a bitch wakes me up every night with his 'Jesus, Jesus, Jesus.' And I'm an atheist. If he thinks he's Jesus, fine, but let him keep it to himself."

Johnston asked, "What do you have to say about this, Smith?"

Smith, of course, didn't answer. Just sat there stone-faced.

"Sorry," Johnston said, "What do you have to say about this, 'Jesus'?"

Smith contemplated the question for a while and then said, in his most sanctimonious tone, "I'm trying to get this ward right with God. I can cure those who believe in me. Those who hinder me are Pharisees and Sadducees."

One of the other patients said, "Say what? What's a fuckin' Faducee?"

Later that day, Smith spent hours seated on his top rack with his arms outstretched along the wall and his head lolling to one side. Patients would go by and say, "Hey, Jesus, how's it hanging?" When anyone approached and gave him a hard time he said, "Forgive them father for they know not what they do. And, besides, they're all mother fuckers."

One day, during the group therapy session, Smith suddenly pointed to the left corner of the back of the ward, just behind the circle of chairs, and screamed. He ran into the corner and fell onto the Monopoly board, which had been carefully placed there by the players when group therapy began. He crushed the board, and the houses, hotels, properties and piles of money scattered.

"You son of a bitch," one of the guys who had been playing earlier shouted. I already had Board Walk and Park Place."

"What is it?" Johnston called after Smith.

"The Virgin Mary is here. Look, oh you unbelievers. Behold my mother."

Everybody looked, but nobody saw anything. "Cut the bullshit, Smith," one guy called. "The only virgin over there is you, and you suck donkey cock."

But a kid who had been admitted to N-2 the day before with an anxiety attack, and had not yet been seen by the shrinks, stood, crossed himself, and screamed, "I see her, I see her. Praise God, I see her." Then he turned over his chair with a loud clattering sound and fell over backwards in a faint. After Kreeg reported the incident to Captain Quarter, this kid's transfer to the open ward was delayed several days. And he didn't last there. Five days later they sent him back down to us. He claimed to be some saint nobody had ever heard of.

"He's no saint," said Wally, who was Catholic. "You need three miracles to make saint. This kid is just crazy."

"Well, isn't saints just crazy people anyway?" said Townsend. Wally didn't like that. "And, besides, why do you have to be a Catholic to be a saint? What about Protestants? Why can't I be a saint? Even Jews like Rock, here?" I thought maybe, for once, Townsend had a point.

Trouble with the Jesus thing accelerated dramatically when another whackjob was admitted to the ward who also claimed to be Jesus. Now we had Jesus #1, Jesus #2, and the kid who had seen the Virgin Mary and said he was a saint was also in the mix— though he calmed down after a while, maybe out of his confusion over which of his two confederates was the true Jesus—and was again sent back up to the open ward.

The new Jesus was a curly haired redhead, tall. He carried the Bible with him and went about the ward blessing everyone—pointedly ignoring the other Jesus. The two immediately had conceived a hatred for one another. Some of that hatred was spawned by the fact that #2 Jesus was Navy, #1 Marines. When #1 said what jarheads are always saying, "*Semper fi*" (always faithful), no one knew whether he was speaking as a marine or as Jesus. Another problem between them was that Jesus #1 claimed to be a Catholic Jesus, while Jesus #2 claimed to be a Protestant one. Jesus #2 allowed that Jesus #1 might be the pope, but he was no Jesus.

Jesus # 1 replied, "I ain't no pope."

"Maybe not," Jesus #2 replied. "Maybe you just like to fuck little boys up the ass behind the altar."

Each Jesus insisted the other was an imposter. Jesus #2 said he was the Second Coming and insisted, "Being as I am the Second Coming, this guy couldn't be Jesus because he was here on this ward before I came, and the first place I came to when I arrived was this ward because I knew how much I was needed here." He also made fun of Jesus #1's attempts to look like Jesus. "Look at those crummy rubber bands," he would say. "In his second coming Jesus isn't supposed to look like Jesus. Scripture says he comes back as somebody else, a redhead like me, maybe even a broad. This other guy is just an asshole."

Jesus #2 was just as crazy as Jesus #1 but quieter and well-spoken, so he was easier to listen to and got along better with the other patients. Also, I was partial to Jesus #2 because he was, like me, a draftee and Navy. When it came to crazy, marines, at least on our ward, were always slightly in the lead.

When the other patients mocked out Jesus #2, he was nonplussed. "We've always known that when Jesus returned he would be persecuted again," he said. "My ministry is among the unbelievers, so this is a good place for me to be."

Jesus # 2 took a ballpoint pen and sketched "J. C." in large letters on the crotch of his pajamas. I happened to be filling out some papers at the front desk when I asked him about this. He said, "This represents Jesus' power. The gospels got it all wrong: it's the e-rection Christians ought to be celebrating, not the res-urrection. Talk about your miracles. If it wasn't for Jesus, we'd all have limp dicks. A hard dick: now *that's* a miracle. One moment it's soft, the next it's a boner. Back then I got laid regular. That Mary Magdalene was some piece of ass, let me tell you. I'd have married the bitch if I hadn't had to do the crucifixion thing. We really got it on. 'Second coming' has two meanings. Lemme show you."

Then, before I could stop him, Jesus #2 took his dick out of his pajama bottoms and laid it on the desk. "What do you think?" he asked. Even not erect, it was enormous. Some of the patients gathered around to observe this freak of nature. Jesus #2's schlong was so long it looked like a snake, like, if he wasn't careful, he might trip over it. And, as one of the patients was quick to point out, "It's circumcised." This gave Jesus #2 a considerable advantage in his competition with Jesus #1—both the size of his much envied penis and the fact that it was circumcised. Jesus #1 came over for a look and scoffed. "Jesus was always known to have an average sized cock because he came from among the common people," he said. "This man's cock proves he's an imposter."

One of the other patients asked him, "How do you know this shit?"

"It's in the gospels," he replied. No one asked him where. When it came to scripture the other patients on

Blueberry Hill bowed to the expertise of the two Jesuses, even though it was obvious they made up gospel on the spot.

The two Jesuses spent much of the day growling and snarling at each other like a pair of nasty dogs. The ward wasn't big enough for both of them. They circled each other, seeking an opportunity to get the other by the throat; they made a lot of noise. "Pipe down, for crissake," other patients would shout.

"Yes," one or both of the two Jesuses would answer, "for Christ's sake indeed."

One day, the two Jesuses got physical. One shoved the other, and soon they were wrestling on the floor and punching each other, the other patients egging them on, laying bets on who would win the fight. Jesus #1 was getting the worst of it. "I'm trying to turn the other cheek," he cried, entrapped in Jesus #2's headlock, "but this son of a bitch won't lay off."

Kreeg and I tried to separate them and I got hit hard in the nose. I didn't know if I was hit by Jesus #1, Jesus #2, or Kreeg. When we managed to pull them apart I was bleeding badly. This was the second time I had been injured on the ward. The blood was everywhere: on one of the Jesuses, on the floor, and all over my Navy white top. "Blood of the lamb," said Jesus #1. He bared his chest and pointed to his heart. "Sacred heart of Jesus," he said.

"Fuck you," said Jesus #2.

"And the donkey you rode in on," replied Jesus #1.

"Your mother."

Kreeg said, "You'd better get that blood off right away, Rock. Cold water."

I went down to the head and washed the blood off in one of the sinks and found a hanger and hung my top in the sun, outside in the recreation yard, hooking the top of the hanger into the chain link fence. I worked the rest of the shift in my T-shirt.

While outside, I got the idea of drawing a line and making sure Jesus #1 and Jesus #2 stayed on their own side of it. Luckily, their racks were already on opposite ends of the ward. Kreeg liked the idea, so I bought a thick nub indelible pen at the PX and drew a line an inch wide on the wooden deck across the middle of the ward. Used up all the ink in the pen. We told the two Jesuses that, except for group therapy sessions, and going to the head or out into the yard, they had to remain on either side of that line. If they didn't they were going into the padded cells for a few hours. Though we usually used the padded cells for dangerous patients, it was also a good way to separate potential combatants, almost like "time out" for kids.

For the most part the two Jesuses followed the instructions separating them, but they did spend hours right at the line insulting each other. One or the other would say, "Get behind me, Satan," but there was no way either could get behind the other since they couldn't cross the line on the floor, though sometimes they got confused and found themselves each on the wrong side of the line.

The line soon served a secondary purpose. A broad jumping competition broke out among the other patients, using the line as their launching point. Soon they had progressed beyond broad jumping and were doing the hop, skip, and jump, beginning a run near the ward front door and launching themselves in their flapping pajamas and slippers from the line I had drawn.

The two Jesuses weren't sure how to comport them-selves during this athletic display. Jesus # 1 had a per-plexed look on his face. Jesus #2, after some hesitation, cheered on the jumpers. He believed not only in the sex-ual but in the muscular Jesus as well. "That's the thing about being Jesus," he would say. "You gotta be a regular guy."

Some of the patients landed badly when they did the hop, skip, and jump, hitting the floor hard with their butts or spraining an ankle. One, quite remarkably, landed on his feet but couldn't stop and crashed into a rack, getting a nasty bump on the head.

Just then Captain Quarter came onto the ward. No one had been aware of his approach until his raspy voice boomed, "What the hell is this? Why isn't this out in the exercise ward? This is a United States Navy hospital ward, not a track and field meet." Then Quarter spotted my line. "And what's this? Who did this?"

Kreeg explained.

Quarter looked at me. He said to Kreeg, but I was sure it was for my benefit too, "Government property has been vandalized."

Oh shit, I thought, *another Captain's Mast?*

But Kreeg must have gotten Quarter to recognize the efficacy of my line in keeping the two Jesuses apart, because he said nothing further about it.

The base Catholic chaplain would show up on our ward once in a while, but when the trouble with the two Jesuses began he came more often. He seemed to consid-er the two Jesuses his professional responsibility. "Blas-phemy," he said. He tried meeting with the two Jesuses in one of the shrinks' offices, but that proved impossible be-cause of the hatred between them. Then he tried meeting with each of them alone. The one thing the two Jesuses seemed to agree on was that the chaplain was definitely Satan's emissary if not the big boy himself. The chaplain did serve one positive function. He drew the warring Jesuses together in a shared antagonism to him.

The chaplain told me he was "very concerned" about the influence the two Jesuses might have on the other patients. I told him not to worry about it. "Even crazy people know a crazy when they see one," I said. "They may even be better at spotting one than we are."

The chaplain told Kreeg, and he passed it on to Wally, Townsend and me, that the two Jesuses were "possessed." He was considering exorcism.

Townsend said, "That would be just great. We don't have enough trouble already? A little exorcism and we'll all go around the bend—not just the patients but the staff too. Jerry Simon," he said mentioning my friend, then working the p.m. shift on the open ward, "is already half way there."

"What are you talking about?" I asked.

"He's starting to flip," Townsend said. "I can always tell."

"Bullshit," I said. But I hadn't seen Jerry in over a month. And that time he had passed me in the corridor of the hospital and nodded, didn't say anything. I had thought then he was just preoccupied. Now I wasn't sure.

Not long after this, Jesus, #2 was air evacuated back to the United States. This surprised me because I had thought he might be a tad saner than Jesus #1. But I remembered that, as with Billy Goldsmith, sometimes the saner seeming ones were the real crazies. With them, crazy wasn't just a stage they were going through, temporary; it was who they were.

As with other patients, we never knew what happened to Jesus #2. But many years later I happened to see a porno movie in a hotel room in Amsterdam and the male star looked a lot like Jesus #2. I wasn't sure it was him, but the guy not only had a huge, circumcised cock; he had red hair. Assuming that was him, I was happy to see he wasn't in a mental hospital and had found some remunerative work. Whether he still thought he was Jesus or not I didn't know. Maybe he did. He had, after all, claimed Jesus got laid plenty, and he sure was doing that.

As for Jesus #1, I had thought that with the departure of his nemesis he would have been in all his glory. He actually was for a few days: no competition. He would be discovered regularly working hard on his stigmata. He walked about saying, "Now it has come true what was long ago foretold. Behold." He would spread out his arms when he said "Behold."

"Behold what, asshole?" one patient said to him.

But then one day I found him back in the corner of the ward where he had seen the Virgin Mary. He was sitting on the floor, crying inconsolably.

"What's the matter?" I asked.

He was too choked up to answer.

"Take it easy and just tell me what's the matter," I repeated.

"I miss the other Jesus," he gasped, letting out a long wail of grief. "I miss him so."

The Therapeutic Community

———— ⚓ ————

Robby Johnston, the psychologist, wanted to extend his notions about a therapeutic community to the staffs of N-1 and N-2. As he put it in a memo to all of the medics: "Only if we work in harmony, can we benefit the patients. Friction between us is reflected in the continuance and even exacerbation of mental disturbance."

"*Mental disturbance*?" Townsend said, "I like that one. Why doesn't he tell it like it is: *Crazy fuckers*. And what's 'exacerbation' mean? Is it what you intellectuals do instead of masturbation, Rock?" I thought Townsend was joking, but you could never tell with him. Was he funny or stupid? Or both?

Whenever Townsend spoke about Johnston, he stuck out his right hand with a limp wrist. "You know what?" he would say. "I think Johnston is a faggot." Of course, Townsend thought everyone working on our ward was a faggot who didn't, deep down, despise the patients. That probably included me. If you didn't hate the patients, you were a faggot or a pussy.

My own feelings about Johnston were mixed. I admired his taking Japanese lessons off base, that he was the only one on the senior psychiatric staff interested in Japanese culture. But I thought his ideas about the wards, especially N-2, were naïve.

Johnston proposed that the entire staffs of N-1 and N-2 meet once a week elsewhere in the hospital "to clear any static among us." He called it "sensitivity training." I'd never heard of such a thing, but by the 1970s it would be affecting human relations everywhere in America. Everybody got "sensitive" in the 1970s. Johnston pioneered it on our ward two decades before, with equally unpromising results. Shortly after people get sensitive, they start smacking each other around.

Johnston proposed that the staff meet on an empty ward where we were not likely to be interrupted. A skeleton crew would be left on both wards—one medic on N-1 and two on N-2, a guy from the night shift and a guy from the a.m. shift. On N-2 no corpsman was to be on duty alone in case of violence between patients or attacks on a staff member. There were many more patients on N-1 than on N-2, but they were not considered seriously ill or dangerous. They were "recovering."

Three o'clock seemed the best time to hold these meetings. The a.m. crew would just be going off duty, the p.m. crew would be coming on, and the night crew could by then have awakened from their daytime slumbers. Between the two wards, excluding the guys who had the day off, we would have about fifteen corpsmen at the meetings, plus Johnston, Nurse Kelly, Commander Robinson, and Captain Quarter.

Quarter was dubious about Johnston's proposal. "Don't we have enough problems with the patients? Do we have to look for problems among ourselves as well?" one of the medics heard Quarter say to Johnston.

Quarter didn't believe in what he called "psycho-babble." He prescribed a lot of Thorazine for the patients on N-2. "Our main job is to keep the patients calm on N-2 and to get the patients on N-1 back to duty as soon as possible," he would say. Johnston thought we could do more than that. He was interested, he said, "in the full liberation of the human soul." Reluctantly, Quarter agreed to go along with him. "But only once," he made clear. "Then we'll see."

Commander Robinson also had his own ideas on what we should be doing for our patients. He didn't believe in using drugs and he thought group therapy was nonsense. He wanted to do psychoanalysis as he had before he was drafted. Since this was impossible on our wards—too many patients—he was eternally frustrated. Also, as a draftee there was a natural antipathy between him and Quarter, a lifer. Quarter took pride in always looking spiffy in his Navy uniform, as if at any moment, psychiatrist or not, he might be asked to take command of a ship. Robinson dressed sloppily, as if the uniform was something he put on only because he had to. Seated at our staff therapeutic community session, he slouched and had a look on his face of sheer boredom.

The session at first seemed to echo the patient sessions on N-2. We sat around in a circle and no one had anything to say. Johnston was disappointed. "Come on," he said, "things aren't perfect; we can do better." No one could argue with that, but I found myself wondering whether leaving well enough alone might be a better idea.

Johnston was democratic. He insisted all corpsmen call him "Robby" rather than "Lieutenant," something that clearly irritated Quarter, who believed rank should at all times be respected. Johnston was also interested in breaking down what he considered "the false barrier between staff and patients. In a way, all human beings on the planet are patients," he would say, "and we can also be therapeutic with one another." He wanted the staff to love the patients and to love one another. "Love" was the key word, he said.

From what I'd seen of the Navy thus far, love had to be in extremely short supply. "I ain't lovin' no patients," Townsend whispered to me. "You guys neither."

I told Townsend that was okay with me.

I admired Johnston's idealism, but I thought tolerance was a worthy enough goal in our circumstances. We were in the military, not nursery school. Spending enough time with crazy people will turn idealistic liberals into conservatives at least temporarily. That was true of me on the ward and since leaving the Navy. After each disappointment with my fellow human beings it takes a while for me to crawl back to my customary liberalism. But, as the joke goes: "a liberal is a conservative who hasn't yet been mugged." Or hasn't worked on a locked psychiatric ward and been exposed to a steady diet of the darker side of life.

Also, did Johnston really think that we corpsmen were going to speak honestly and openly with Captain Quarter present? As a draftee it didn't much matter—I was putting in my two years and getting out—but for lifers like Kreeg, whose welfare and promotions depended on Quarter, it was naïve to think they were going to speak up about anything of substance. Johnston would appreciate it, but Johnston had little clout. If Kreeg complained about anything, the fitness report from Quarter at the end of the year calling him "a whiner" would probably be his reward.

Johnston kept pushing. "I just know we have things to talk about," he said. "And let me be clear: whatever is said here stays here. Nobody gets in trouble no matter what they say. You can criticize or offer suggestions to anyone; I have Captain Quarter's word on this. In here, forget rank. We all want the same thing: the successful healing of our patients."

Still silence.

Perhaps to relieve the tension in the room, two of the medics who presently worked the N-1 a.m. shift, had something to say about Jerry Simon, my old buddy from boot camp and hospital corpsmen school. I was glad to see Jerry at the meeting, but apprehensive. Townsend had mentioned something about him being "shaky" but I rarely paid much attention to anything Townsend said. I smiled a hello at Jerry, but he didn't smile back. That was puzzling.

A kid named Bobby Rowe said, "I want to talk to Jerry Simon. Jerry, you came on the ward yesterday and didn't say anything to me. Not hello, not good morning, nothing. And it wasn't the first time. You mad or something? What'd I do?"

Jerry didn't respond.

"Look," Rowe said, "We could work better, Jerry, if you were friendly. The lieutenant's right: the patients need us working together."

Still silence, but Johnston beamed. Something was happening, so that was good.

The other guy who worked with Jerry, Will Thornton, said, "I agree with Bobby. Come on, Jerry, what's the problem?"

I didn't think Bobby and Will had a serious beef with Jerry Simon. I suspected they were mostly looking for ways to score points with Johnston if not with Quarter as well.

Johnston was vigorously nodding his head in approval. "We don't judge anyone here, Jerry. We're here to help one another develop our humanity to the fullest and, also, to improve patient care."

Jerry just sat there staring straight ahead. Time ticked by. Maybe Townsend was right about Jerry being "shaky."

Johnston cleared his throat. This therapeutic community thing was his baby; it would be an embarrassment if it didn't work. I noticed that Quarter, rolling his eyes, his mouth tight, was looking at Johnston with an expression that suggested, "I don't have time for this."

"Jerry," Johnston said, "how about the following? Tell us what you're feeling right now. Doesn't matter what it is. Anything will do."

Everyone would agree later that this was a bad suggestion. Had Johnston left Jerry alone, hadn't pushed, perhaps whatever was bothering him would have blown over.

But it was too late now; Jerry felt under attack. Suddenly, he stood up and screamed, "I'll tell you what I'm feeling right now, mother fuckers. I'm feeling like I can't take any more of this shit." And, with that, he ran out of the empty ward into the main hospital corridor.

For a moment we all sat there, frozen. Then Captain Quarter shouted, "What are you waiting for?" so we got up and, en masse, ran out into the corridor. Had Jerry turned left or right? Someone spotted him running far down on the right, and we took off after him, yelling his name: "Jerry! Come back, Jerry! Jerry!!" It was ridiculous. We were chasing one of our own staff members, but what else could we do? Jerry Simon had gone around the bend.

I was fast, had once competed in track, so I led the pack. There we were, the whole Neuropsychiatric gang—fifteen corpsmen, a nurse, a psychologist, and two shrinks, eighteen of us altogether, chasing a colleague down the main hospital corridor who was screaming back at us, "Mother fuckers! Mother fuckers!!"

I felt sheepish running after my friend. Also, I didn't know what I would do with Jerry if I caught up to him.

Suddenly, Jerry reached into a case in the wall and removed a fire extinguisher. Lifting it over his head with both arms, he heaved it at us. In effect, he heaved it at me because I was out front. The fire extinguisher hit the concrete deck with a deafening, clanging sound and rapidly rolled towards me. I timed my jump over it, but it hit a crack or bump and bounced up and hit me in the shin. The blow knocked me down, followed, a moment later, by excruciating pain. I thought for sure my leg was broken. Everyone charged around me, continuing after Jerry.

Jimmy Kreeg finally tackled Jerry by the door to N-2. With Jerry thrashing about, Kreeg held him down as best he could and yelled, "Get a straightjacket for crisssake." Since none of us ever took our keys off ward, we couldn't open the door. Robby Johnston knocked loudly. One of the guys we'd left on duty opened the door, sheer bewilderment on his face. "Quick, a straightjacket," Johnston said.

"For who?" the guy asked. He thought we had all lost our minds. Why did we want a straightjacket out in the hall? Why was Jimmy Kreeg wrestling with Jerry Simon? This guy was used to following procedures. There was no procedure for this.

"Get the fucking jacket," Johnston said, as Jerry Simon continued to wrestle with Kreeg and two medics who had piled on. This was the only time I ever heard Johnston use the "f" word. Until then, virtually everyone but him used it regularly.

I had by now discovered that my leg wasn't broken; I was just in terrible pain. Hobbling down to join the others, I watched Jerry in a straightjacket being carried into our ward horizontally by three of the medics. He looked like a dead guy wrapped in a shroud, except that he was still kicking.

"Put him in a cell," Captain Quarter said.

Some of the corpsmen from other wards, having heard the commotion—the sound of rushing feet, the many voices calling after Jerry Simon, Jerry's screams— had dashed out into the corridor and witnessed the drama, relishing the sight of the entire psychiatric staff chasing after one of its members. This proved that you *did* have to be crazy to work in psychiatric. Then there was me getting hit with the rolling fire extinguisher "You'll never make it as a basketball player, Rockland," a black medic from another ward told me later. "You jump like you suffer from white man's disease." There was the added irony of Jerry being tackled by Kreeg right in front of N-2. And then there was Jerry, a staff member, wrapped in a straightjacket and carried into the locked ward.

For months to come this event would be rich fodder for making fun of those of us who worked in psychiatric. Everyone knew our N-2 patients were "crazy." Most of them ended up as Section 8s—guys discharged from the military for "mental incapacity" or worse. But chasing a wild eyed staff member down the hospital corridor also suggested that the gulf between our staff and our patients was, as corpsmen from other wards had long believed, not wide. When the other medics saw N-2 staff members from then on, they didn't only have "Blueberry Hill" to make cracks about. Now they would say, "Hey, Section 8, howya doin'?"

The patients on N-2 also were astounded to see a psychiatric staff member come through the front door wrapped in a straightjacket, screaming, and put into a padded cell. They noted our whole staff craning our necks to see inside Jerry's padded cell through the small observation window. Staff members of a therapeutic community, Johnston had said, "must speak with one voice." The patients could plainly see that this was not true.

One patient, a schizophrenic, started screaming, "It's the end of the world," his screams in counterpoint with Jerry's. Another patient went running at full tilt to the far end of the ward and, perhaps to punish himself for some imagined indiscretion, crashed into the wall. Then he got up and did it again.

It was as if the Jerry Simon incident had placed the security of our patient's world, limited as it was, in jeopardy. They had to believe that we, the staff, knew what we were doing and now, as they could see, we didn't.

Jerry was still screaming. "Get me out of this fucking straightjacket," he shouted. Kreeg looked at Captain Quarter and, when he nodded, Kreeg opened the door and he and a couple of other guys got Jerry out of the jacket and handed him pajamas. He threw them at them.

They beat a quick retreat but not before Jerry said, "Some friends you guys are. I'm a medic, goddamit. Why are you treating me like a fucking patient?" Everyone stood around feeling guilty, especially me.

"Okay," Captain Quarter said, "break it up. Whoever isn't on duty on N-2 now get off the ward." He added, "Lieutenant Johnston, I'd like to see you upstairs in my office immediately."

Apparently the behind closed doors discussion Quarter had with Johnston was animated. Or so the on duty staff of N-1, who could overhear some of it, reported. They heard Quarter shout and Johnston plead. Apparently, Johnston was arguing that what had happened with Jerry was an aberration, that one more attempt at a therapeutic community meeting of the staff should be made. Quarter was having none of it. "Enough of this horseshit, Lieutenant. We tried it once. That's it." When Johnston came out of Quarter's office his face was deep red.

As for Jerry, he was now a patient on our ward. It was weird for all of us having a colleague as a patient, but worst for me. That patient was my friend. Things got even worse after Jerry was let out of the padded cell and was walking around in pajamas and had been assigned a rack. He refused to attend the group therapy sessions, just sat on his rack. None of the staff said anything to him about it, not even Johnston.

We didn't know how to deal with Jerry. Nor did the other patients. They stayed away from him, didn't trust him, thought he might be a spy from the staff. Jerry walked around all day enraged. He hated being one of the patients. And he hated everyone working on N-2 for keeping him one.

"We were friends, Mike," he said to me. "Get me out of here."

"Believe me, I would if I could, Jerry," I said. "But look: the best thing would be to just calm down. Stop acting like you hate everybody, like you're 'crazy.' Act normal and soon you'll be on N-1 and then maybe back to work."

"I want out of here now. Just leave the door open a second, Mike."

"You know I can't do that, Jerry," I replied.

"Yeah, then fuck you."

Jerry kept saying, "Okay, I got mad. Big fuckin' deal. When can I get out of these pajamas and back into my uniform? When do I get my job back?"

The answer, unfortunately, turned out to be never. After a couple of weeks Quarter had Jerry air evacuated back to the United States. We wondered why he was sent home so quickly. I had imagined he would almost immediately be transferred to the open ward and would soon go back to duty—perhaps not in psychiatric, but surely he could be useful elsewhere.

Maybe Quarter had his reasons, and Jerry was seriously ill. I didn't think so. I had taken a look at Jerry's chart. There in Quarter's handwriting were the words "paranoid schizophrenic." I didn't believe that for a minute. I just thought Jerry was an embarrassment. A staff member Quarter supervised had flipped. Maybe the Jerry Simon story had trickled out of the hospital and reached the admiral's desk. Maybe Quarter was covering his own ass by getting Jerry out of sight as quickly as possible.

Since Jerry had been one of us we were eager to know what happened to him, and someone on N-1 found out and let us know. Jerry had been discharged from the Navy as a Section 8. None of us told the corpsmen on the medical wards what had happened to him.

I continued to feel guilty about Jerry, as if I had personally let him down. I managed to get his address in the U.S. and wrote him a letter, told him how sorry I was, but he never answered. He didn't answer a second letter either.

Robby Johnston was in a funk after the incident with Jerry. His ideas had been discredited. It wasn't that the patients were like us; it was that we were like the patients—at least one of us was. And, we thought, if Johnston kept going with his therapeutic community, we might all end up like Jerry Simon.

Johnston was also in the doghouse with Quarter. He kept the daily group therapy sessions with the patients on both wards going, but that was the first and last time a staff session was held. "Shit," said Townsend. "I was kinda looking forward to seeing which one of us would flip out next."

"Probably you," Wally said.

"Me?" Townsend said. "Hell, man, I ain't ever going to flip out, you know why? Because I hate this fucking place. That makes me immune."

"You don't give a shit," I said.

"Exactly right," Townsend said. "If you want to stay sane in this man's Navy—especially in the fucking locked shrink ward—that's the first rule: 'don't give a shit.' Look at that sorry assed Johnston. He wants us to love the patients. Love 'em? This is war on N-2: us versus the patients. We don't watch our asses these fuckers will get us."

I didn't want to agree with Townsend but there was some truth in what he was saying. The lesson I had learned in boot camp was operative on N-2 also: you had to turn down your feelings and always be wary. If you didn't, you might go nuts or someone might get you. The latter would prove true sooner than I expected.

Friendly Fire

— ⚓ —

"Therapeutic Community" or not, N-2 could be a dangerous place to work. Though it was peacetime, twice in my months there I came close to, as they say in the military, "buying the farm." As mentioned earlier, I saw combat on N-2.

The first time involved another patient escape. It began to dawn on Kreeg, Townsend, Wally, and me one morning that patient Joe Louis Jackson, a strong black kid diagnosed as paranoid schizophrenic—accurately diagnosed; not like Jerry Simon—was not on the ward. Neither the front nor the back door had been opened since the four of us came on duty except to let the food cart in with breakfast.

"He must have gotten out then," Kreeg said, but Wally was sure he had seen Jackson after breakfast, and I thought I had too. Perhaps the patients knew something but we didn't want to discuss it with them, didn't want to reveal our concern. It might undermine our authority; give them ideas of themselves escaping.

The laundry cart hadn't come on the ward yet so Jackson's absence couldn't have anything to do with that.

Besides, he was too big; he would never have fit. So, where could he be? And if he was missing, who would take the rap this time? Not me, I vowed. If I got in trouble again, the admiral had said, the penalty would be severe. "Let's find him," Kreeg said. "If we do, we keep quiet about it, like it never happened; if Quarter hears about this, the shit will hit the fan."

We quietly searched the ward. Nothing. But in the head I noticed something: the grate that covered the air duct in the ceiling was slightly askew. Was it possible Jackson had climbed up there somehow, twelve feet up, pulled the vent up with him, and gotten it almost perfectly back into place? That seemed impossible, but Jackson was a frogman, technically an underwater demolition specialist. Those guys preceded the Navy Seals, who came along in 1962.

The other patients called Jackson "The Human Fly" because he had once made his way down the ward by all but walking along the wall over the racks, getting toe holds here and there. Everyone applauded. If he had escaped through the ceiling of the head, you could see where he might have gotten a start by climbing atop one of the urinals. But how did he get above that point, fly? It was seven feet from the top of the urinals to the ceiling, so he possibly could have leaped from the urinals, but the urinals weren't directly under the air vent. Had some of the other patients boosted him or let him climb to the top of a pyramid? One of the patients had been a cheerleader in high school. Could he have organized a pyramid? Unlikely, what with four of us on duty in that small ward, however distracted by other concerns.

Kreeg knew of a rickety but very tall wooden step ladder that leaned against the wall in one of the vacant wards, used occasionally for changing ceiling light bulbs. He sent Townsend for it. The ladder was worn and dusty, must have dated from when Yokosuka was a Japanese base. Kreeg also got hold of a flashlight. The flashlight in my pocket, I climbed to the top of the ladder, skipping a rotten step along the way. Kreeg held the ladder steady. I handed down the grate and peered inside the duct with the flashlight. Nothing, but the duct extended far off into the distance. I tried to boost myself up into the duct but couldn't get a purchase on anything. And even if I had, I didn't want to crawl inside that duct. It was deep in dust and, I thought, probably too narrow for me. I'd get stuck. I had once tried spelunking and lasted five minutes before I freaked out from the claustrophobia. The duct would be worse, especially if Jackson was in there and wanted to fight.

"Call him," Kreeg suggested. I felt a little ridiculous, but I yelled "Jackson!" over and over down that long, dark duct. A couple of patients wandered into the head to see what all the commotion was about. They stood around, amused. Anything that made the staff look bad was a source of pleasure to the patients. If we screwed up, it made them feel better about themselves. Townsend told them to "Fuck off!" When they didn't move, Kreeg added, "Now!"

I yelled "Jackson!" a couple more times down the duct. My magnified cry, bouncing off all that metal, boomed like a chorus of bassoons. About to give up, I heard laughter. Jackson was indeed in there somewhere. "Come and get me, mother fuckers," he yelled.

I shone the flashlight again. I couldn't see him, but I could just make out what looked like a trail through the dust. Then I saw that there were junctions in the duct where it branched off in several directions. Jackson must be down one of those side ducts.

"Joe Louis," I called, "come out of there." I remembered that he always wanted to be called "Joe Louis," not just "Joe." Sometimes he actually thought he *was* Joe Louis, the boxer. We had had our two Jesuses, and now we had our Joe Louis.

"Come out," I repeated.

"Wouldn't and couldn't," was his reply, his voice booming as mine had.

"Why?" I called.

I didn't make out what he said about "wouldn't," but "couldn't" was clear: "you can't turn around in this son of a bitch."

Then Jackson asked, "Is Kreeg out there?"

I told him that he was.

"Tell him to go fuck himself," Jackson called. It seemed Jackson really had it in for Kreeg.

"He says to go fuck yourself," I told him.

"If we don't get him out of there, "Kreeg said, "I might just have to do that."

Wally volunteered to go in after Jackson. Being black he thought he might be able to effectively talk to him where the rest of us couldn't. He replaced me on the ladder and managed to hoist himself up into the beginning of the duct. But he was too chubby. He only got a foot or so in. "Shit," he said as he backed out, his face covered with grey dust.

What to do? We couldn't just leave Jackson in that vent. Who knew when Quarter might drop down to N-2 and ask what was going on? Also, what if Jackson died in there?

Assuming we could figure out which branch of the duct he was in, where did it lead? To the furnace? To another ward? It was impossible to say. If we knew where it led we could just sit and wait till Jackson came out that end. Otherwise, extricating him might involve taking half the hospital apart.

Kreeg phoned down to the hospital's main office. "Do you have plans of the building, specifically the duct system?" he asked.

The Japanese probably had such plans but their whereabouts were unknown, Kreeg was told.

"Wally," Kreeg said to Barker, "you stay here in case he somehow backs out. Towny and Rock, you look after the ward. Pretend nothing's happened or, at least, that everything's under control. I'm going to learn what I can outside."

Kreeg was gone half an hour, but he came back with news. Jackson was now up on the roof. One of those duct branches apparently led to a vent in the ceiling of the staircase to the roof. Jackson had crawled that far, removed the vent, and dropped down; Kreeg had found the vent lying on the staircase. He had climbed to the top of the staircase but couldn't get the steel door to the roof open. Either Jackson had bolted it from the outside or placed something extremely heavy against it. Kreeg had banged on the door and shouted, but Jackson ignored him.

"Okay," Kreeg said, "here's what we do. I stay here because the guy hates me for some reason. Rock, you go out and talk to him. I don't think he has anything against you. If he won't come down, see if you can get him to let you up on the roof via that staircase. No other way up there. Towny, you stay here with me, so we have two on the ward. Wally, you go outside with Rock but stay out of sight. Two guys and he feels threatened. If he'll let you onto the roof, Rock, Wally goes too but stays back, listening good. Rock gets into trouble, you're his backup. That kid is strong. Take a straightjacket with you."

Outside, I could see Jackson on the roof silhouetted against the sun. "Joe," I called.

"My name is Joe Louis," he reminded me, "not Joe." I assured him I would never fail to call him that from now on.

"Well, whatya want?"

"I want to talk."

"Go ahead and talk. I can hear you."

"No," I said. "I want to come up there and talk face to face."

"What about?"

"Whatever you want to talk about."

"Yeah, well I got nothing to say to you," he said.

I kept at it, hoping to wear him down. Maybe if he got bored enough with our conversation he would let me up there. Time was passing. It would be impossible to keep Quarter from knowing about this if I didn't talk Jackson down soon. I wondered whether he had had his breakfast before escaping; maybe he was hungry.

"How about some food?" I called up to him.

"Whatcha got?"

"Whatever you want."

"Okay, I want three eggs, sunny side up, bacon, rye toast, home fries, and a pot of coffee. Cream and sugar."

I told him it would take a while. "I'm not going anywhere," he said.

I went into the hospital mess hall, Wally trailing me. The cooks took some convincing. "Breakfast is over," they said.

We told the top chef that this was an emergency. "What kind of emergency?" he wanted to know. I said "Top Secret." "Bullshit," was all I got by reply. Wally backed me up. "You don't do this," he said, "your names are in the report. We're talking court marshal. You'll wish you never were born." I was impressed with Wally's inventiveness.

The chef stared at us. We stared back. "Okay," he said, "but just this once. When the mess hall is closed, the mess hall is closed." We readily agreed that this was so.

Fifteen minutes later I was ascending the staircase to the roof, balancing a large tray in my hands. Wally was the better part of a flight behind me. I winked at him before kicking the roof door several times. "That you, Rockland?" I heard Jackson say in a muffled voice.

I told him that it was.

"You alone?"

"Yes."

There was the sound of something heavy scraping across the roof surface and then the door opened. I walked out into the sunshine and handed Jackson the tray. I tried to keep the conversation light. "Man, did you really crawl all the way out through the ducts?"

"Sure did," Jackson said, proudly.

"Phew," I said, thinking a compliment might help. "You underwater guys are really something."

Jackson shrugged. He was covered head to toe with dust. But dust or not, he was hungry. He sat cross-legged on the roof eating and I sat across from him. I noticed something about this roof I didn't like. It was entirely flat with no parapet around it.

When Jackson had finished eating, I made my move. "What say we go down now, Joe Louis?" I said.

"Is that why you came up here?" he asked, turning nasty.

"Joe Louis, it's my job. You belong on the ward."

"You trying to say I'm crazy?

"Not at all," I replied, trying to reassure him.

"Well then, why do you mother fuckers have me on a nut ward?" he said.

"I don't know, Joe Louis. Maybe they made a mistake. But the longer you stay up here the more serious this gets. If we go down now nobody will say anything."

"Yeah, you'll put me in a padded cell."

I didn't know if I had the authority to say this but I assured him: "No padded cell. No nothing. If we go down now nothing will happen to you. Things will be exactly the way they were before. That's a promise. I just have to take you down with me."

The words "take you down" seemed to set him off. "Take me down?!" he yelled.

"You and what army? I'm a frogman."

"Doesn't matter if you're a 'whaleman,'" I said thinking some levity might calm the situation.

It was a dumb thing to say, especially given Jackson's heroic sense of himself. In a rage, he leaped on me and we were wrestling on the roof.

He wasn't so much bigger as he was stronger than me. Much stronger. And he was trained in martial arts. Any moment I expected a blow to the neck. Why the hell had I come up here?

Jackson didn't hit me, but he got me in a full nelson. He was pressing down hard, and I remembered that, with enough pressure, you can break someone's neck. Now, from behind, he was walking me towards the edge of the roof. Either way I'm dead: broken neck or off the roof. Where the hell was Wally? I tried to kick back at Jackson's legs but didn't connect. The pain in my neck was excruciating, and we were getting closer to the edge.

"Help!" I finally yelled. "Help!" It was the only time in my life I've ever yelled "Help!"

I couldn't have been more than five feet from the edge when Wally came at Jackson from the side with such speed and force that he knocked him off me and fell on top of him.

But Jackson was only temporarily stunned. He was coming out from under Wally. Now he had Wally in a full nelson and, with both of them on their knees, he was pushing Wally towards the edge. The son of a bitch was probably stronger than Wally and me put together.

It was simply instinct. I ran across the few feet between me and them and, with my plain black Navy right shoe, as hard as I could, kicked Jackson's head as if it was a football. Thunk. It was a sickening sound. Jackson went flat, knocked out. I could have cared less; it was him or us.

Jackson wasn't going to be unconscious for long. Wally had dropped the straightjacket as he crossed the roof, so I fetched it and we wrapped Jackson up in it. Luckily, he was still groggy from my kick. We each took him under one of his arms and half walked, half dragged him, off the roof, down those flights of stairs, down the hospital corridor, and up to the door of N-2.

"I'm going to report you, Rockland," Jackson said before we entered the ward. "You kicked me in the head. You can't kick a patient in the head. That's brutality."

"You go right ahead and report it," I said. At that point I didn't give a damn what he did; I was just glad

Wally and me were alive. Luckily, perhaps out of pride, Jackson never told anyone he had been vanquished on the roof—not that I know of anyway.

At our knock, Kreeg opened the door, with Townsend just behind him. The four of us hustled Jackson into a padded cell.

"You said no cell," Jackson screamed.

"Yeah," I said. "But that was before you tried to kill me and Barker." We closed and bolted the door, leaving him in the straightjacket for the present.

After we turned away from the cell, Kreeg said quietly, "We're keeping this to ourselves, agreed?"

Townsend said, "Fuckin' A."

"I'm not writing a report," Kreeg added.

"Roger that," Wally said. "We gotta watch our own asses, because ain't nobody else gonna watch 'em."

I told Kreeg and Townsend that Wally had saved my life. Wally said, "Well, you saved mine too." Wally and I were really close after that. Maybe not as close as I had been with Billy Goldsmith—something I wanted badly to forget—but Wally had the considerable plus of not being crazy.

I came close to getting killed a second time a month later. Wally and I were on night duty together, 11:00 p.m. to 7:00 a.m. Only two corpsmen did night duty because lights out was at 11:00 and the patients usually slept through the entire shift. I both liked and didn't like night duty. I didn't like having to stay up all night and then trying to sleep during the day. I did like that, having nothing to do, I had plenty of time to read at the desk at the front of the ward. Sometimes Wally and I played chess, but mostly we read. He appreciated my recommending books to him. "This Hemingway can write," he said.

One night Wally and I were reading when he needed to go to the head. I nodded and he disappeared down the dark ward with the flashlight we kept in the desk drawer. The ward was especially dark with the blinding light of the desk lamp in my eyes. I could see nothing but the book I was reading, so I never saw the patient creeping up on me after Wally went to the head.

Suddenly someone had me by the neck from behind. I fought to pull his hands off my throat, but they were big hands and strong. My struggles were useless, and I couldn't make a sound. I remember thinking this is it: I'm going to die before Wally gets back from the head. I'm gonna...

That's all I remember until Wally was saying, "Easy, Mike, stop it." The beam of his flashlight was in my eyes. I was no longer on the little platform on which the desk stood but twenty feet away. I was on top of somebody and repeatedly banging his head against the wooden deck. I had ahold of his ears and was using them as handles to smash his head against the floor as hard and as fast as I could.

"Stop it, Mike," Wally yelled, "you'll kill him." He turned on the overhead lights in the front of the ward.

Unconscious beneath me was the guy everyone called "Gunny." He was big, had played offensive lineman in high school. After that he had been a much decorated gunnery sergeant in Korea. He was the typical patient—a guy who had been a hero, stayed in the military, and, in Japan, with nothing to do, went nuts. He was in our ward for observation because he had pointed a loaded .45 at another marine for no reason anyone could determine. And now he had tried to kill me. I had no memory of how I got him off me and how we ended up twenty feet away from the platform.

I got up. My heart was pounding and I was freezing. My teeth were chattering in the warm Japanese night that seeped through the barred windows. "What happened?" Wally asked. "I don't know," I replied. "I was reading and suddenly I'm being strangled." "But how'd you get him off you?" "Haven't a clue. He's choking me at the desk and next thing you're telling me to stop banging his head against the floor. I don't know how I got him off me or how we ended up over here." "Adrenalin," Wally said. "Maybe so," I said. But it was weird. One minute I'm being strangled, the next I'm banging the guy's head against the floor. And no memory of how he and I changed places so that, by the time Wally came along, he wasn't killing me, I was killing him. This was the second time Wally had arrived just in time to save my life—or more likely Gunny's life by that time. "Damn, Wally," I said, "if you're going to save people's lives, can't you get here a little sooner?"

"I was constipated," Wally said.

Later that seemed terribly funny, but just then I said: "Yeah, a little more constipated and somebody would have been dead." Maybe me, but probably Gunny because if Wally hadn't stopped me I might have kept going till Gunny's head was pulp.

I had been totally out of control, had experienced for the first and only time in my life what it is to be insane. I startled giggling. Then I started crying. And I was still freezing. "Get me a blanket please, Wally," I said.

Wally got me a blanket and said, "You're in shock."

"Yeah," I said, "tell me about it." All I wanted was to go off somewhere by myself and cry for a long, long time.

These days there's much talk about military personnel "placed in harm's way." I served in the Navy in peacetime and twice came close to being murdered—but nobody ever said anything about my being "placed in harm's way?"

I wondered what the Navy would have done with me had I killed Gunny. Would they have believed me when I said Gunny attacked me? Maybe they'd have thought I attacked him. Either way, if I had killed him, would it have been murder? Manslaughter? Self-defense? How would I be able to prove "self-defense?" My having no memory of how we got from the desk to the floor all that distance away wouldn't help in any judicial proceeding. Not to mention that my only witness was Wally, and he hadn't seen Gunny strangling me; he had only seen me smashing Gunny's head against the deck.

We had to do something about Gunny, who had opened his eyes and was looking around. For all I knew the son of a bitch would start strangling me again.

But now he was a pussycat. Barker got a straightjacket and Gunny didn't resist as we put him in it. But he did ask, "What did I do?"

"You tried to kill me, that's what you did," I said. "You strangled me."

"Why would I strangle you?" he asked. "You're not the enemy. You're not even a gook." I wondered if, by "gook," he meant Japanese or his mind was back in Korea. Either way, he had a look of total disbelief on his face.

Gunny didn't have anything against me. That night he'd have strangled anyone sitting in that chair with the light in his eyes. There was nothing personal in it. "You're not the enemy," he repeated.

"There is no enemy," I said.

"No enemy?" he said. "How can there be no enemy? There's gotta be an enemy."

It was as if his whole existence depended on there being an enemy. Without an enemy, life had no meaning to him. "No enemy?" he said again, looking so sad I almost felt sorry for him.

Life's simple in combat: you kill the other guy or he kills you. No complications. Gunny was a combat junky, and in Japan there wasn't any combat so he made himself some. With me.

I was myself high on "combat" just then. The shock was fading, and what was taking its place was a certain satisfaction that somehow I'd beat this big marine in hand to hand combat. But it went beyond that. I was happy to think of myself as a warrior, as tough. I ever so much wanted to know how I had gotten Gunny off me, but I didn't know and never would. I was proud anyway. Sure, it was a macho thing, but so what?

Wally was saying something, but I wasn't listening. Then I tuned in. He said that we had to have Gunny examined medically. Maybe I'd fractured his skull. Maybe he was hemorrhaging. But first Wally asked, "You okay, Mike?"

"Fine," I said. I didn't want Wally to know just *how* fine. "Let's get this guy looked at."

But with only two of us on duty we couldn't leave the ward. Wally phoned X-ray and the tech agreed to come down for Gunny with a gurney. "Just keep him in that straightjacket and, when I get there, we'll strap him down. I'll find the radiologist and have him come in. We'll have a look at his head. How'd he get hurt?"

Wally said, "We don't really know. We found him banging his head against the floor."

I expected Gunny to refute what Wally had said, but he didn't say anything.

He probably didn't know what to believe at this point.

"Thanks, Wally," I said later. "Quick thinking."

For the next hour or so Wally and I sat in our chairs by the desk talking. I was too distracted to read.

The X-ray tech brought Gunny back and said, "Nothing. The doc says no skull fracture, probably just a concussion." In those days, nobody worried much about concussions. "His ears…one of them was half torn off—but the doc stitched him." Sure enough, Gunny had a bandage on one of his ears, looking like Vincent van Gogh after he cut off part of his ear.

"How'd the ear happen?" the tech asked. "I gotta do a report."

Wally and I shrugged.

For safety's sake, we put Gunny into a padded cell for the rest of the night. We took off the straightjacket and he lay there looking up at the ceiling. I should have been more professional, but I couldn't resist crouching over him and repeating, inches from his face, "*Semper fi* you son of a bitch." That's what marines and ex-marines always say, *Semper fi*. Whenever I hear it, to this day, I feel like throwing up. "I shit on your *Semper* fi," I continued. "What are you faithful to, Gunny, besides trying to kill me?"

Wally grabbed my shoulder. "Come on, Mike, let's go." He was right. I felt like a bully saying what I did to Gunny. And now I could see that he was crying, the tears running down the sides of his face onto the mat floor. He had nearly killed me, and I hated him, but I felt sorry for him too, the poor, miserable son of a bitch.

Before the a.m. crew came on duty, we got Gunny out of the cell. He seemed foggy about the events of the night. I was a bit foggy about them myself. There's a tiny part of me, maybe one percent, that has always wondered whether I might have attacked him rather than him attacking me. *No*, I tell myself, *that's ridiculous*. But there'll always be that tiny smidgen of doubt. How *did* I ever get that big guy off me?

Wally and I debated whether we should report what had happened. After all, if Gunny did this once he might do it again. On the other hand, we were both afraid I might find myself in serious trouble. Still, what was to stop Gunny from sneaking up on me or someone else another night? We decided that, while we were on night duty, we would never leave the other alone even for a second. We'd do everything in tandem: patrol the ward together; always be at the front desk together; go to the head together, one doing his business, the other waiting just outside.

Later, we told Kreeg and Townsend about our idea and Kreeg said, "Good plan." He passed the word and that's what everyone did from then on when on N-2 night duty.

On balance, Wally and I decided to report the incident with Gunny. First, when the a.m. crew relieved us, we went to the hospital mess. I ate a huge breakfast, as if experiencing the flip side of having your last meal before being executed. After breakfast, we went upstairs to see Captain Quarter.

Quarter listened to the whole story without interruption and then said, "Good thing you didn't kill him, Rockhead." If he felt any concern for me whatsoever, he didn't express it.

"What if I had?" I couldn't help asking.

"You would be shit out of luck. We don't kill our patients. Now, let's just forget it. You're not hurt and the sergeant's not hurt badly either. Best we forget it."

"A report?" Wally asked.

"No," Quarter said. "Forget it means forget it." If you could ignore something in the Navy, you ignored it. That too was "The Navy Way."

But Quarter didn't ignore it for long. Three days later Gunny was taken from the ward. He was air evacuated back to the United States, manacled to an armed guard.

I wasn't sorry to see him go; he had nearly killed me. But he and I had experienced the ultimate together, a life and death thing, so, I felt a strange kinship with him. I doubted he would remember me, but I would never forget him.

"He'll be all right," Wally said. "After a while they'll let him out of the Marines. Nobody will care that he once pointed a gun at another marine and strangled you and, besides, they'll never know about him and you because there's no report. Wouldn't surprise me if, because of his record in Korea, they give him an honorable discharge. They'll have to: he's got a Purple Heart. Got nicked in the ass in Korea. Not much more than a mosquito bite, three stitches."

"That's rich," I said. "I got wounded more than that by that Blueberry Hill kid—six stitches. Joe Louis Jackson nearly killed you and me both. And now Gunny almost kills me but he's the one with the Purple Heart."

"That's right," Wally laughed. "No Purple Hearts for friendly fire."

Off the Base

⚓

As mentioned earlier, N-2 was not much larger than a stage, and everything that happened on it was dramatic, even theatrical—that is, when it wasn't terrifying. It was inevitable that when I left the ward some of it went with me, so I had to be careful that, like Jerry Simon, it didn't stick to me.

Outside the hospital there was plenty to distract me, even on the base. There was a decent library and a photo shop where I learned to develop and print my own pictures. You could shoot pool, see first run movies, the food in the mess hall was decent, and my quarters in the barracks offered a reasonable amount of privacy—though I certainly would have liked to have a fourth wall with a door instead of just a three sided plywood cubicle. While at Yokosuka I completed two correspondence courses in American literature with the University of Maryland overseas program, prerequisites for graduate school, and they took up most of my off-duty time.

But I also needed to get off the base. Wasn't that why I had fought so hard to get to Japan, to see the country? I also figured that I needed to regularly get away from the military. Townsend, who usually got it wrong, put it best: "You work on N-2 and stay on the base too much you go bugfuck."

Townsend didn't much follow his own advice. He was one of the guys who virtually never left the base except to get laid in Yokosuka. He had no interest in the Japanese, hated them even. It had nothing to do with World War II. He just didn't, as he put it, like "slant eyed people, slopes. They're sneaky," If there had been a McDonald's or some other outpost of American civilization in Yokosuka he'd have gone there regularly, but he wanted nothing to do with the Japanese, Japanese culture, or Japanese food.

Besides, like the rest of us, he was told, "Never eat food off the base." We were regularly told stories about personnel who had eaten Japanese food and, afterwards, were intestinally crippled for weeks or even months.

It was a little like the warnings in boot camp about fraternizing with prostitutes. Still, most of the single men on the base and those coming off ships went to prostitutes regularly; there were no other women. It was extremely difficult to meet a nice Japanese girl with whom you might have a real relationship, assuming you wanted one, and they figured that there were always the pecker checkers to take care of their venereal diseases. They were less afraid of catching a venereal disease than of eating in town.

I always ate Japanese food when off base and never got sick. Japanese food was much better and more interesting than Navy fare. And the Japanese seemed more concerned with sanitary conditions than we were.

Almost immediately after my Captain's Mast penalty had expired, I began going on trips on my day off.

For the first one I rented a Fuji Rabbit brand scooter at a place just across the street from the base's main gate and rode up into the terraced rice paddies of the hilly countryside inland from Yokosuka. The Rabbit made me think the Japanese had a thing about rabbits. We look at the moon and see the man in the moon; they see a rabbit, its ears trailing off to the right. One legacy of my time in Japan is that, to this day, I see both.

When I rented the scooter, nobody asked for any kind of license, so I just went. However, the further out into the countryside I got, the more worried I became about making it back to Yokosuka, since I spoke little Japanese and couldn't read the signs.

Japanese farmers, men and women—the men in straw hats, the women with polka dot kerchiefs on their heads plus hats—were working the paddies. They looked at me curiously as I rode by. One man was carrying buckets of night soil and spreading it over the fields. I wondered why this plentiful supply of fertilizer, treated, isn't utilized in the United States. Cow shit and horse shit are okay, but human shit is not? I didn't get it. I still don't.

I was passing slowly through a village on a narrow dirt road when the scooter slid out from under me on a sandy spot. I fell off and banged up my left knee. My jeans were torn, and I was bleeding. Two women came out of their thatch roofed houses, and with much chattering, kindly put some liquid on my knee which I took to be disinfectant and bandaged my knee. Their children stared at me as if I was a Martian. I wondered if the kids had ever seen an American before. One of them kept pointing at me and saying a word in Japanese that I later learned meant "big nose." I don't think I have a particularly large nose, but I guess I do by Japanese standards.

After many smiles and thank yous and bows, I continued on my journey. The two women were much better at the bowing than I was; they had more practice. Aboard the scooter, my lower back now hurt more than my knee. I decided not to return the scooter but to rent it on a long term basis. I kept it chained to a lamppost outside the barracks. On my next day off I headed in the direction of Yokohama and wandered into a large bathhouse where everyone—men, women, and children, from the same families or perfect strangers—were naked and bathing in the naturally hot pool into which water bubbled up out of the volcanic earth.

After some hesitation, I paid a small fee, stripped, and joined the Japanese in the pool. It was a novelty being naked with perfect strangers, though the sulfurous water smelled like rotten eggs. The Japanese seemed to have an entirely different attitude than Americans about nudity. I had already learned that Japanese public toilets were everywhere coed—though difficult to use: no seats in the stalls, just a hole in the ceramic fixture on the floor. So you had to squat uncomfortably and, when you flushed, you had to jump out of the way of the rushing water.

Nudity and sex did not seem linked in Japanese minds. I thought this a healthy thing. I wondered what the Japanese would have thought of *Playboy*, which had already been published for a couple of years and was sold in the base PX, the first of what would prove to be a blizzard of American skin magazines. *Playboy* constituted a revolution. Until it appeared, the only place you might see women's breasts in magazines was in *National Geographic*—native women in Africa or the South Pacific, not the blond "girl next door" *Playboy* featured.

In addition to their attitudes towards nudity, the Japanese seemed to have a passion for cleanliness. They were almost too clean. Did they never sweat? I learned from Robby Johnston that the Japanese thought Americans smelled badly and attributed this to our large consumption of beef. On public conveyances in Japan—buses, trains—no matter how crowded, one noticed no body odor whatsoever. I wish one could say the same for the New York City subways. Also, the Japanese were always so neatly dressed they looked like they had just stepped out of a laundry or tailor shop.

They did everything in a prescribed manner. A Japanese tea ceremony—I went to more than one in Yokosuka—was done just so. It was a spiritual experience, a meditation. First you bowed. Then you sat on the tatami floor. You didn't just slug down the tea. First you had to admire the pot from which it was poured. Then you had to admire the ceramic cup into which your tea had been poured by charming geishas. The cup had no handle, so you held it in front of you in both hands at arms length. When you raised it to your lips you made appreciative noises. Smacking your lips was not bad manners; it was expected.

The Japanese were also unfailingly polite, excessively so by American standards. Everything in my limited exchanges with them seemed to be about not losing face—neither theirs nor mine. I could understand bowing once when meeting someone. It would be like shaking hands. But I never had a conversation with Japanese people—me with the few Japanese words I was picking up, them with their few English words—in which bows weren't repeated endlessly. And the Japanese were always smiling, as if not to do so might be considered an affront. They seemed to smile whatever the subject or situation was, so I wondered. Were their smiles genuine? Townsend had a thought on that: "the fuckers are laughing at us."

I didn't think that was true, but I wondered whether the Japanese smiled so much to maintain a certain distance between people. If an American smiled at me all the time, I would think he was trying to con me or sell me something I didn't want.

One evening off base I went to a Japanese sumo wrestling bout in Yokosuka. I couldn't make head or tail of it. Two hugely fat guys wearing nothing but loin cloths bowed and then paced about in a circle making grunting noises before grappling with each other. All the other Japanese were trim; one saw no one overweight in Japan and certainly no obesity. But these sumo wrestlers must have weighed four hundred pounds each. I didn't understand sumo wrestling but, whatever was going on, it wasn't fake like American professional wrestling.

My favorite place to go on my day off was the small city of Kamakura and its Great Buddha. Forty-four feet high, forged of bronze in the year 1252, it once had a temple surrounding it that was carried away by a tsunami, but the Buddha itself hadn't budged. The Buddha is so large you can climb inside it from the back. I had no interest in doing this because it was the Buddha's face that intrigued me, that strange, enigmatic face that seemed, perhaps because of my western eyes, to simultaneously express infinite love and infinite disdain—or maybe the two cancelled each other out and the face was simply expressionless. If so, perhaps the absence of expression was supposed to suggest true enlightenment. I have no idea, but each time I went to Kamakura I stared at the Buddha's face by the hour, transfixed.

What was the Buddha telling me? It seemed as if he had passed beyond the central, unresolved issue in western religions: the question of evil. If God is good and God is great (all powerful) why does a little child die of cancer? If God is good and God is great, why are there earthquakes that devour thousands of people? If God is good and God is great, why were six million Jews murdered in the Holocaust? Perhaps the Buddha was telling me that there was nothing to tell me; that the western religions with their heaven and hell and saints and miracles were just wishful thinking. Or to put it another way, perhaps the Buddha was telling me that the obsession in the West with morality and immorality and with a personal God was what kept human beings from reaching a higher plane. It was as if he was wearing one of those T-shirts that say "Shit Happens."

I wondered what the Buddha would think of the morality of the United States Navy—of the right way, the wrong way, and the Navy way. Perhaps the Buddha offered a fourth way.

I went regularly to Kamakura on days off and just stood there looking up at the Buddha. It was a meditation. The Buddha wasn't doing anything, and I wasn't doing anything either. Americans always say, "Don't just sit there, do something." Perhaps there is greater wisdom sometimes in the reverse. "Don't just do something, sit there."

Sometimes I stood so long staring at the Buddha I attracted attention. Once a policeman wandered over and surreptitiously checked on me, kept circling around me. I guess he was making sure I wasn't up to no good. Or that I hadn't lost my mind. No, I would have told him, if I had had enough Japanese, I may have found my mind.

I would return to the base and ward N-2 after each visit to the Buddha with a deeply peaceful feeling. It wouldn't last, but it was worth going to Kamakura anyway.

My experiences off base were about to increase dramatically. I received a letter from my wife confirming that she was coming over to Japan for a couple of months during an extended break from college.

But where would we live? Base housing was only for officers and chief petty officers and their families. Happily, I learned that we were allowed to live off base. I spotted a notice on a bulletin board in the hospital's main office that a medic named Bob Benjamin, who worked elsewhere in the hospital, was looking for someone to take over his lease for two months; he had been living off base with his wife and was leaving to go state-side.

On my day off, Benjamin took me out to see the house. We boarded the train at Yokosuka station and got off at Zushi. From there we took a local bus that seemed to stop at every corner en route to the Isshiki Beach neighborhood of Hayama, where the emperor's vacation palace is located. Indeed, Benjamin's little house backed up against the great stone wall of the palace. It looked almost like the emperor's wall was holding it up. If I took the house the emperor would be my "neighbor," I mused, and the wall surrounding his palace would almost be like a shared party wall.

The inside of the house was spotlessly clean. This was because, as Benjamin explained to me, you never wore the same footgear inside Japanese houses as out. There was a little stoop at the entrance, and there you took off your outside shoes and put on slipper-like shoes for the interior of the house. The Japanese, indeed most Asians, consider Americans barbaric because we wear the same shoes in our homes as we do in the street—which of course makes our houses filthy and in constant need of cleaning.

There was little furniture in the house because the Japanese mostly live on the floor. They eat on very low tables while seated on cushions, and they sleep on the floor. The floors in the house we would inherit were mostly of light yellow tatami, which has a beauty all its own and is wonderfully soft underfoot. Only the kitchen and bathroom had wooden floors, and in the center of the bathroom, in addition, to a western flush toilet with a seat (Hallelujah!), there was a round bath over four feet deep. You bathed standing up. No shower.

The interior doors of the house, called shoji, were made of light wood and rice paper. They slid rather than operating with doorknobs and hinges. And while providing privacy, they let light through. There was also a special place in the house, an alcove called the takanomo where you placed something exquisite—a perfect vase, a bonsai plant, some lovely smooth stones—a kind of shrine, not to God but to beauty. Perhaps, I thought, they are the same thing.

What a pleasure it would be for me to leave the grey, ugly naval base and the locked psychiatric ward, where everything was hard and cruel, and come out to this pretty and soft little house and my wife. The long commute would be well worth it.

I met the landlord, who lived with his family across the alley in a much larger house. The front of it was a grocery store; the family lived in the back, sleeping on their futons. This was long before futons became common in the United States. I wonder whether all Americans who use them know that this way of sleeping comes from Japan.

After a good deal of smiling and bowing and tea drinking the landlord agreed that I could take over the remaining months in Benjamin's lease. He kept saying, "No problem." These seemed to be his only English words. I would hear those words often over the next months. The rental for the house—hard to believe—was $25 per month in yen.

Neither then nor in the months to come would I ever learn my landlord's name. He tried "Rockland" and gave up. The Japanese turn the "l" into an "r" and vice versa, but the landlord couldn't handle "Lockrand" either. "Micu" seemed to work for "Michael" and we got by with that. When the landlord addressed me he added on the honorific. So I was "Micu-san."

I was excited about the house. My wife would be coming and I would get a chance not only to live with her but to actually live in Japan when I wasn't on duty. Luckily, two months on a.m. were coming up, the best shift for regularly returning home to Hayama. I was glad I had held onto the scooter. I would ride it to Zushi, eliminating the need for that peripatetic bus, and there lock up the scooter and jump on the train for Yokosuka. I would live like many in the United States, a commuter with "the little woman" out in the suburbs.

My wife arrived at Yokohama by ship. The irony did not escape me that I was in the Navy and had never been aboard a ship but she had.

She found the little house in Hayama, our first home, charming, and I was pleased with myself for finding it. She, much more than me, would be living in Japan full-time, and this showed as she quickly picked up Japanese, surpassing the little I had.

The only trouble with the house we soon learned were the occasional appearance of bugs of colossal size. Bob Benjamin had not mentioned them, and I had not seen any when I examined the house with him. In the bathroom black water bugs three to four inches long sometimes appeared. When they did, I had to smash them with a shoe, take the remains outside in a dust pan, and then wash off the dustpan and the bottom of my shoe with the landlord's hose.

Worse were the spiders. These were almost the size of my hand and didn't just crawl. They jumped from wall to floor and then onto another wall with a zinging sound. Luckily, I was home when my wife saw the first of them. She screamed. I came running from the bathroom where I had just killed a water bug. "What..." I began to say, but she just pointed in horror.

The spider she was pointing at was on the wall, and so big I momentarily thought it must be one of those rubber spiders you can buy in a novelty store in the United States to scare your friends and wondered why my wife had put it there. Didn't I have enough trouble with the water bugs?

This was the dinosaur of spiders, a mutation out of a science fiction movie. How had it entered the house? What made killing it and its brethren especially challenging was that they didn't hang out in the bathroom or kitchen where, at least, there were hard surfaces against which to smash them. They frequented the parts of the house that had soft tatami floors and thin walls and shoji doors. If I smashed a spider on a shoji door with my shoe it would break the delicate structure and wouldn't even kill the spider. It might have been possible to kill one on the tatami floor with repeated blows, but it would have left a terrible stain. Mainly what I did was shepherd the spiders towards the bathroom or kitchen—all the while fearful they might turn and leap on me.

I called both the water bugs and spiders to our landlord's attention (brought a dead one of each to show him). He laughed and said, "No problem." But there *was* a problem. I gestured to him with the bugs and he laughed and again said, "No problem." I said, "Yes, problem," but he laughed and said, "No problem." It was hopeless. At the base library I got out a book titled *The Entomology of Japan* and learned that neither the water bugs nor the spiders were poisonous nor did they bite. But they were still horrible to look at and live with.

The giant bugs problem did put a crimp in the ability of my wife and me to enjoy our little house. And it was worse for her. She was there most of the time. I, at least, went to the base six days a week. The bugs problem made even N-2 somewhat more attractive simply because, however ugly, at least it didn't have crazy bugs, just crazy men.

Despite the occasional appearance of both kinds of bugs, we enjoyed the novelty of our little Japanese house, and the charming neighborhood we were living in. It was fun just to stroll about it, though wherever we went the Japanese stared at us. We were the only Westerners living in Hayama as best as I could determine.

Our favorite thing was to go down to Isshiki Beach—just walk along, sometimes employing the excellent binoculars I had recently purchased to look out to sea. One day on the beach we noticed a contingent of armed police, stationed every twenty feet, some with heavy weapons. They looked at us suspiciously. Out to sea, about two hundred yards offshore, was a man in a little rowboat surrounded by three Japanese destroyers. Training the binoculars on him, we saw that it was Emperor Hirohito. I had read somewhere that his hobby was oceanography and that he often went out in a glass bottomed boat. The scene was cartoon-like: this little bespectacled man surrounded by great grey warships that utterly dwarfed him and his little boat. It was hard to believe that this man had been responsible for, or had certainly acquiesced in, Japan spreading so much misery and death throughout Asia and the Pacific not many years before.

Not long after my wife arrived, we decided that it would be nice to invite our landlord and his wife over for dinner, show them some traditional American hospitality. It took a long conversation and lots of hand signals to communicate what we had in mind but we seemed to get the message across because, on the appointed day and hour, they came across the alley between the two houses dressed in their finest (Mrs. Landlord wearing a kimono) and carrying indoor footwear with them, though we had some ready for them.

Ten or fifteen minutes went by while we made pleasantries in our respective languages—which neither side understood—and did a great deal of bowing and smiling.

When it was time for dinner, we sat on cushions on the floor around the beautiful lacquered black table, six inches high, which was the only purchase of any consequence we had made for the house. It was intimate having dinner like that, though I would never come to tolerate sitting without back support. I eventually shipped that table back to the United States. It arrived undamaged, but after six months in the drier, so much less humid precincts of Minnesota where I went to graduate school, the table developed a large crack down the middle, and then one day it split and toppled to the left and right, its four little legs straight up like a dead animal's. There was no remedy except to throw it out, but doing so hurt.

Although no one said much during the meal, and of that little virtually nothing was understood, my wife and I counted the dinner a success. Later we would wish it had never taken place. The very next morning the landlord was waiting for me in the alley as I prepared to mount my scooter and head for Zushi and the train to Yokosuka. He began in the usual way—lots of smiles and bows—and then began to say something I did not understand. I was going to be late for work, so I called my wife outside to talk to him and roared off. That night I learned from her that our landlord had expressed the desire for us to come over to his house for dinner some day soon.

She had thanked him profusely, tried to tell him that having us over was certainly not necessary but we were delighted to accept and would be looking forward to the occasion.

The following day, when I returned home from the base, my wife told me that as she went out the door to shop that morning the landlord was waiting for her and they had the identical conversation. "Well," I said, "I guess he really wants us to come."

But the following day, as I was mounting my scooter, the landlord appeared again (he seemed to be watching for either of us as we came out the door) and, as best I could determine, he repeated the same invitation. I smiled and bowed and thanked him, and as I rode off wondered why he kept inviting us. We had already said we would be more than happy to come.

The next day my wife said that that morning she had again had what was fast becoming "the conversation" with our landlord about our coming over to dinner and, although this was becoming a bit irritating, she thanked him and communicated as best she could that we would be delighted to come.

"Why does he keep talking about it?" I asked her.

"I don't know," she replied. "Maybe he's just being polite."

But in the ensuing days it didn't seem polite at all. The same conversation took place with one or the other of us every day. So much so, that even I had come to understand his words. Well, at least I was picking up some Japanese.

But I said to my wife, "I'm getting sick of this. Why doesn't he just have us over or forget it?"

"It's a mystery," my wife said.

Perhaps so, but the "mystery" continued day after day after day, the same ridiculous conversation.

"This is torture," I said. "Why doesn't he just do it or shut up about it? I am fast losing interest in going over to his house. He's starting to bug me more than the bugs."

We began to avoid the landlord whenever possible. I would race out the door, jump on my scooter, and tear out of the alley before the landlord could accost me. Sometimes, in the rearview mirror, I could see that he had come out of his house and just missed me.

But, of course, he would get to my wife later in the day. She had often shopped at his store. Now she went to other stores. And when she left the house she walked as fast as she could, almost ran, to get out of the alley before the landlord appeared. But sometimes he would run af-

ter her down the road and the conversation would be repeated with all the bowing and smiling that went with it.

"Maybe we can just tell him to forget it," I said.

"I wouldn't know how to say that," my wife replied.

"But I feel like I'm being harassed, almost stalked."

"Me too," I said.

"Yes, but you escape on your scooter to the base."
We then had an argument because she thought I should
handle my share of the conversations with the landlord.

"I can't let him make me late for N-2," I said. "I'll get
in trouble on the base."

"Well, then go out there five minutes earlier and give
him a chance to say it to you."

So I did it the next day and that night I said to my
wife, "If this keeps up I'm going to strangle that son of a
bitch. What the hell is this? World War II all over again
and this time the Japanese are winning by driving us crazy? This guy is a sadist. He can take his dinner and shove
it up his ass."

Nevertheless, the daily ceremony continued. When
it was my turn, while the landlord talked and we smiled
and bowed, I took to saying things in English I figured he
couldn't understand. It made me feel better to say these
things. "Well, fuck you too," I would say with a big smile.
Or "I'm going to get me a Samurai sword and cut your
balls off if you don't stop torturing us," I would say with
an even bigger smile. I needed to do this. It was therapy.

The landlord's routine continued. Earlier, I had
come to understand what he said; now I could have said
it myself.

The end of the two months was quickly coming to a
close, and my wife was returning to the United States and
college. On our last day in the little house, we were pack-

ing the taxi that would take my wife back to Yokohama and the ship that awaited her. No surprise: the landlord appeared and he went into his spiel, but it was slightly different this time. What he said, as best we understood it, is that when we *returned* to Japan he would have us over to dinner. All the rest of the words were the same, but the "returned" part was different.

We did our best to smile and bow and assure him that nothing would make us happier when we returned to Japan than to come to his house for dinner. Of course, it wasn't likely we would be in Japan again. And in case we were, we knew that we would rather starve than go over to his house for dinner or put up with his infernal invitations.

I rode with my wife as far as Zushi. We were both sad to leave our little home—landlord, giant bugs and all—but breathed a sigh of relief as we pulled away. We had loved that little house, but the landlord had made us miserable with his insufferable invitation. I said to my wife, "If ever I return to Japan and find myself in Hayama, I'm going to kill that guy."

"Do it slowly," she said.

I do wish I could have known who the new tenants were going to be so I could warn them never, *ever*, to invite the landlord and his wife over to dinner. But looking back on our time in Hayama years later, with the safety of the United States and the Pacific Ocean between the landlord and me, I'm glad the whole thing happened. It was like some wonderful shaggy dog story, insufferable but memorable. I've been married to a different woman for many years now, but the experience with that landlord is something, on the rare occasions I see her, that my first wife and I still laugh about.

Years later a possible light was shone on the mystery of the landlord and his invitation. I was in conversation with a scholar at the university where I teach whose specialty is Japan. He told me that what my landlord had done was much more than respond in kind to our invitation to dinner. By not having us over, he remained in our debt for life; having us over would have discharged that debt. "You're seeing it from an American point of view," this Japan expert told me. "Can you imagine how tough it was for this Japanese man, every day, to go through this little ceremony? Believe me, what he did was tougher on him than it was on you."

I didn't believe what this scholar said and still don't. It sounded like the biggest bunch of malarkey I'd ever heard. And, besides, I'm not letting that landlord off the hook no matter what strange customs he had. If he wanted to remain in our debt for life, he could have found a way of doing it that didn't torture us. Just not inviting us would have been fine. Let the cultural anthropologists weep. Tolerance of cultural differences goes just so far.

Death on the Psychiatric Ward

———— ⚓ ————

L iving off base with my wife, and experiencing something of Japan, proved to be only a temporary escape from the terrors and absurdities of N-2. My own brushes with death were soon paralleled by other traumatic events in the psychiatric wards: two patient deaths. This was beyond strange. Patients die on medical wards—heart attacks, cancer, accidents, wounds, whatever—but one doesn't think of patients as dying while in psychiatric wards. Mental illness isn't fatal unless you kill yourself.

I was involved in some way with both deaths—the first peripherally, the second directly. So I remember them almost as poignantly as my own two near misses.

Jonathan Shelby, a handsome black kid, was admitted to N-2 as a heroin user. It was hard to believe that he had been on heroin; he just seemed too bright, too with it. But there were track marks on his arm.

I got pretty close to Jonathan and, unlike Billy Goldsmith, Jonathan wasn't crazy. He ate. He drank things besides black coffee. He didn't smoke cartons of cigarettes or eat razor blades. After the Goldsmith debacle,

I had sworn to never be friends with patients again, just friendly, but I went much further than that with Jonathan which, later, I would regret because of the sadness it brought me.

I wasn't worried about getting tricked this time because there was no mystery about Jonathan's ailment or why he was admitted to our ward. I had no plans to go see Captain Quarter and tell him there was nothing wrong with Jonathan. There was definitely something wrong with him or had been: heroin. But I didn't understand how he could be brought into our ward, cold turkey, and not have the shakes or be vomiting or all the other things I thought happened to people on heroin when they suddenly quit. He just quit and that was that.

I asked Jonathan about that. He said his use of heroin had been recreational. "I've never been an addict," he said, "but here in Japan it's so cheap, and it gave me a breather from the Navy." Jonathan absolutely hated the Navy, more even than I did. "Racist pigs everywhere," he said. He told me that in boot camp they had given him the nickname "Whitey."

"Why 'Whitey?'" I asked

"Just to fuck me over," he said.

Jonathan was a college grad and a draftee, like me. He came from an accomplished family, his father a professor at Hofstra University, his mother a lawyer in Manhattan. Jonathan had graduated with honors in history from Amherst College. The Navy had offered him the same deal they offered me in boot camp: Officer's Candidate School and an extra year. Like me, he had turned them down.

I was naturally drawn to Jonathan. He was someone I could talk to, and I guess I was the guy on the ward he could talk to. We talked about politics and history and literature and art and about Japan. Whenever I came back from my day off traveling somewhere in Japan, Jonathan wanted to know all about it. I told him about my landlord, and he roared with laughter. He also had been to Kamakura and, like me, was transfixed by the Great Buddha and intrigued by its face. "Yeah," he said, "you don't know looking at him whether he just absolutely, unqualifiedly, loves you or plans to eat you for lunch. That face is pure ambiguity." For both of us, the Great Buddha represented much that intrigued us about Japan.

Jonathan would say, "Man, what am I doing on this nut ward with all these crazies?"

"Heroin's serious business," I would respond. "How'd a guy as intelligent as you get into that?"

In reply, Jonathan would shake his head and say, "Everybody fucks up somehow. This was my fuckup. It was helping me get through the Navy. But no more. It's too dangerous, and I've got things I want to do with my life."

I was rooting for Jonathan. I wanted him to get out of N-2 and onto N-1 as soon as possible and then, perhaps, be sent back to duty. It was important to me that Jonathan complete his two years in the Navy and not receive a dishonorable discharge—which could have screwed up his life. He had all the talent and smarts in the world. He grew up on Long Island, so I imagined getting together with him as friends after we were both out of the Navy. He planned to go to graduate school, get a Ph.D., teach college, and write books. So did I. It would be nice if I was able to take away one good friend from my experience in Yokosuka.

After a few weeks on N-2, Jonathan was transferred to the open ward. I was glad for him, but I missed our regular talks. He was, well, a brother. Sometimes I would ask the guys on N-1 how he was getting along and they'd tell me, "Just fine. Good kid."

A couple of times when I was off duty I visited him on N-1—for my sake as much as for his. In all the time I was in Japan that was the only time I ever visited a former N-2 patient on N-1. It wasn't frowned upon; it was just something no one did, partly because, after an eight hour shift on N-2, all you wanted was to get out of the hospital. But Jonathan was my friend; when I went to N-1, I wasn't visiting him as a patient.

I learned one day that N-1 was now allowing him the freedom of the base during daytime hours. I've never liked bowling but Jonathan came down to N-2 one morning, knocked on the door, and said, "Let's do it," so we went bowling that afternoon when I came off duty. It was nice to be doing something together and to see my friend back in uniform instead of pajamas. Jonathan whipped me good in the bowling, doubling my score. My balls mostly ended up in the gutters.

I learned that Jonathan was soon going to be given evening liberty in Yokosuka one night a week. He was slowly returning to normal life. The next step would be a return to duty.

But his going into town worried me. Every temptation was there, including heroin. I thought maybe I should go with him, keep him out of trouble. The night of his first liberty I was off duty and offered to go with him. I tried to make it sound like I wanted to go myself, not for his sake. I didn't want to suggest he needed "babysitting."

But Jonathan must have sensed where I was coming from. "Thanks," he said. "Maybe next time we'll go together."

I didn't buy his logic; I thought it made sense the other way around—the first time with me, the second alone—and told him so, but he was insistent. How I wish I had gone with him whether he liked it or not, tailed him if necessary.

I stayed in the barracks and fretted. I really started to worry when the medics on N-1, knowing we were friends, phoned me to say that Jonathan hadn't returned by the 10:00 p.m. curfew and asked if I knew where he was. I didn't, and the call creeped me out. I didn't sleep much that night.

In the morning Jonathan's body was brought to the hospital. He had been found in an alley in Yokosuka, the hypodermic needle still in his arm. One of the medics on N-1 later told me that if you've been off heroin for some time, and you get a sizeable jolt of it, it can kill you. It killed Jonathan.

But I knew none of this until, while working morning shift on N-2, a call came from Pathology.

"Are you Hospitalman Third Class Rockland?"

"Yes, Sir."

"We need you at the morgue. We've got a body here, just came in. The corpsmen on N-1 say you're the guy who knows him best. We need him identified. No next of kin here; you'll have to do."

Until then I hadn't even known the hospital had a morgue or where it was. Walking there I mumbled a prayer of sorts: "Please don't let it be Jonathan. Please don't let it be Jonathan."

But it was. The first dead person I ever saw was lying naked on a stone slab. Part of me thought it couldn't be Jonathan. First, I had never before seen him naked, and people look different with their clothes off. Then there was the fact that much of his dark color had drained from his face and body, as if someone had opened a spigot or pulled a plug and all the color had run out. He was a sickly beige with some bluish accents. There was also the simple fact that dead people rarely look the way they did when they were alive unless the embalmers have pumped them full of chemicals. I kept thinking, *this thing couldn't be Jonathan; it's a plastic statue.*

"Is this Jonathan Shelby?" I was asked.

"Pretty sure," I said. I could hardly admit to myself that that thing on the stone table was Jonathan, that the guy I had liked so much, who was full of creativity and energy, had become what I was now looking at in horror.

"Well, is it him or not?"

I nodded. I couldn't speak. I supposed it was better that I was there to identify Jonathan than his poor family. I remembered what they looked like because Jonathan had shown me the pictures in his wallet—his mother, his father, an older brother, a younger sister. It was strange standing in for them. And there was the wallet, sitting on a desk a few feet from the slab, with whatever else he had on him when they found him—a handkerchief, some yen, the hypodermic syringe and needle, his dog tags. The thought that they were probably going to stick one of the dog tags into his mouth, using the grooves for his teeth, sickened me still more.

But that was nothing compared to what was to come. With an electric saw the pathologist began to saw off the top of Jonathan's head. Bits of bone flew, bits of gore. A burning smell filled the room.

I said, "Can I go now, Sir," but the pathologist didn't hear me what with the noise of the saw, so I remained in place. In the Navy you didn't just leave when in the company of an officer. You had to be dismissed. I didn't know if anything further was required of me, so I stayed put.

The pathologist lifted off the top of Jonathan's head. There was his exposed brain. I suppose they needed to access his brain to determine the exact cause of death, though certainly they knew. Or, if not, they could simply have analyzed the remnants of what was in that syringe.

Now the pathologist grabbed hold of the top of Jonathan's face and, with a sound like tearing canvas, pulled it down to his chin, turning his face inside out, his features inside and nothing but a bloody horror where his face had been. Why were they doing this? I had thought they only needed access to his brain. I began to retch.

"Sir," I insisted, "can I go now?"

"You still here?" the pathologist said matter-of-factly.

I ran out the door into a toilet just outside the morgue and threw up. And threw up again. Then I washed my face, went outside, sat on the grass and cried. I was supposed to go right back to N-2, but I needed some time and the other three guys were on the ward. I cried because of the sheer waste of Jonathan's life, but I also cried because I had lost a friend.

I was angry with myself for not insisting on going into Yokosuka with Jonathan no matter what he said. Tough love, in other words. Even if I had made a pest of myself and he had been angry with me, I should have gone. I knew I wasn't by any stretch of the imagination responsible for his death, but I would forever afterwards feel that I might have saved his life. I started to write a letter to his family but then tore it up. There was nothing to say or, at least, I couldn't say it.

The other death happened right on our N-2 ward, and this time I definitely bore some responsibility— though I suffered far less than I did over Jonathan. This death didn't involve someone I knew and cared about. It happened during my second tour of night duty, this time with Townsend. He and I had been sitting together at the front of the ward, the light in our eyes, me reading, he listening to Armed Forces Radio, the volume turned low, when there was a loud knock on the door of N-2. I literally jumped. It was 2 a.m. Nobody ever knocked on the door of N-2 at such an hour.

Townsend and I went to the door together. Outside, Admissions had a skinny little guy on a gurney. He was raving.

"What's the matter with him?" I asked.

"D. T. s" the Admissions corpsman said, handing us the guy's chart, "Delirium Tremens." Apparently this sailor, whose name was Jean Pierre something-or-other, was off a French warship that had put into Yokosuka harbor. The French had no facilities in Yokosuka and had asked if our hospital would hold onto Jean Pierre while he dried out. Their ship was going elsewhere for a week and would pick him up on the way back.

Jean Pierre, a totally wasted alcoholic, was imagining bugs crawling all over him. He kept scratching himself and screaming something in French. He apparently knew no English, and none of the three of us standing there knew more than couple of words in French. I could conjugate some verbs; that was about it.

Townsend said, "Let's put Frenchy in a cell. The fucker's going to wake up the whole ward." Townsend had more experience, so it was his call. And what he proposed seemed reasonable enough. The guy was a drunk. It never occurred to me that he was physically ill; I just thought of him as a guy who drank too much and, so, was not deserving of any particular concern. Alcoholism wasn't looked at then as a disease but as simply an indulgence. Drunks weren't sick; they were just jerks who drank too much.

Jean Pierre's being so skinny should have been the giveaway that he was malnourished and dehydrated. In fact, his condition should have told Admissions that he didn't belong on N-2; he belonged on a medical ward with IVs in both arms. Since we didn't deal with medical cases, we assumed he would be all right after he had slept it off.

If only there'd been a doctor on duty in Admissions at 2 a.m. Surely, he would have put the French guy into a medical ward and hooked him up to IVs. But only corpsmen were on duty at that hour. What they saw was a raving lunatic, so they figured he belonged on N-2.

But had I been paying full attention, this was one time when those sixteen weeks of hospital corpsman school back at Bainbridge might have come in handy. I might have recognized the symptoms even if Admissions and Townsend didn't and insisted Jean Pierre be admitted to a medical ward. I don't know if I would have succeeded, but at least I'd have tried. I never said a word. It didn't occur to me that our hospital was doing something terribly wrong.

We took the French sailor off the gurney and put him in a cell. But he wouldn't be quiet, kept rolling about and screaming. Townsend grabbed him by the throat and shouted, "Shut up, motherfucker." I'm sure Jean Pierre didn't understand what Townsend had said but, sufficiently frightened by him, he quieted down. We locked the cell door, figuring he would go to sleep now.

During the night I read the Frenchman's chart before filing it for the shrinks to see in the morning. There was his picture, in which he looked decidedly better than when he came onto N-2. I could make out enough of the material the French had turned over to know that he was thirty-three years old and had a wife and three children back in France. There were also pictures in his wallet of his family.

Townsend and I never discussed the heat in the padded cell. Without air conditioning, it was 90 degrees and 90 percent humidity in the ward. Bad enough. But it was probably over 100 in the cell and more humid as well. Here was a guy who needed to be hydrated and was close to zero on electrolytes. Instead, he spent the night sweating.

Townsend and I were just happy he had piped down. We thought we had done the right thing, for him and for the rest of the patients: got him to be quiet, got him to go to sleep. In the morning he would be taken out of the cell, given some breakfast and instructed in the ward's ways as best as possible, given the language barrier. We discussed whether he should be included in the group therapy sessions.

"Can't hurt," I said. "If the cats go, he might as well go."

Our relief came on the ward at 7 and Townsend and I were about to leave when we remembered. Townsend said, "Oh yeah, there's a guy in the cell. A Frenchy. A drunk. You should take him out."

The senior guy relieving us said, "Hell, you put him in there, you take him out. You should have had him out before we came aboard."

So Townsend and I opened the door to the cell. Jean Pierre was asleep. We hauled him to his feet. He obviously didn't know where he was or how he had gotten there. And why were these people speaking this strange language? He was terrified, his eyes wild.

We walked Jeanne Pierre out into the ward, Townsend on one side of him, me on the other, holding him up by his arms. We hadn't gone more than a dozen feet when he went totally limp. Little and skinny as he was, he was still heavy, so Townsend and I laid him down on the floor on his back. Townsend got a glass of cold water and threw it in Jeanne Pierre's face, but he didn't move, didn't show any sign that the cold water had affected him in any way.

The senior medic on the relief crew got down on his knees and put his ear to Jeanne Pierre's chest. "Holy shit," he said, "this guy is dead."

None of us did anything but just stare. This was before CPR was commonly known; it had certainly not been taught to me in hospital corpsmen's school. This was also before there were defibrillators everywhere that could shock a heart back into action. If someone's heart stopped, it stopped, that was it. They were dead and there was nothing anyone could do about it. Not in our hospital anyway.

The senior guy in the relief crew told Townsend and me to carry Jean Pierre's body back into the padded cell. "No sense upsetting the patients any more than they are."

He followed us into the cell. "Okay," he said, "pull down his pants."

We did so and he tied a piece of string around the Frenchman's penis with a tight knot. "Okay," he said, turn him over.

We did that too and he began pushing cotton up the dead French sailor's skinny little ass.

"What's this all about?" I asked.

"We don't want him leaking all over the place," he replied. "Okay, now you guys can go. We'll call the morgue."

Townsend and I were relieved to get off the ward. I felt numb, but we went to the mess hall and had breakfast together. Townsend kept saying, "Holy shit. That French fucker is dead. Holy shit."

I fully expected there would be some kind of inquiry, some kind of hearing about this death at which I would be asked to testify, and since the Navy has to blame someone for everything, it was possible that I was in deep trouble. Maybe all of us: Townsend, Admissions, and me.

But nothing happened. Apparently Jean Pierre's body was taken down to the morgue, put in a cold drawer, and kept there until it could be turned over to the French, and nobody said anything.

Naturally, I was relieved that no charges were brought. This French drunk had died. "So what?" seemed to be the official attitude. He had drunk himself to death. That's what the report said. I had a glance at it. It said "Death by acute alcohol poisoning." This wasn't quite true, but no one wanted to look into the circumstances of his death. To do so would have been to admit that our hospital had totally fucked up. But I know, and will always know, that we killed that guy—killed him by admitting him to the wrong ward and killed him by putting him into a stifling padded cell with no provision to hydrate him and get electrolytes pumped into him. And I would always know that there was a woman and three kids back in France who had lost a husband and father forever, and that it didn't have to happen and that I was partly responsible.

I talked to Kreeg about it. He said, "Just forget it. It happens."

"But we made this happen," I said. "This isn't the right way or the wrong way. And if it's the Navy way, it's criminal."

"Maybe so," Kreeg said, "but if you want to cut your throat, I'm not helping you do it. Like I said: 'forget it.' Consider yourself lucky this guy was French. If it was one of ours, there'd be an inquest, and then maybe they would fry your ass. Yours, Admissions, and Townsend's, that dumb hillbilly fuck." This was the first and only time I had heard Kreeg reveal how he felt about Townsend—which was essentially the same way I felt about him.

"The French?" Kreeg continued. "They're probably going to be happier carrying him back to France in the ship's cold storage than having to deal with his drinking and his craziness. So everybody's happy. Leave it alone Mike. You mess with this and I guarantee: the Navy will fuck you every which way it can. And I'm not talking Captain's Mast. This thing's got Court Martial written all over it."

Okay, I was only twenty-one by that time and had had little training and even less experience that would have caused me to insist to the guy from Admissions that this was, at least initially, a medical case, not a psychiatric one. And it never occurred to me to question Townsend's judgment about putting the French guy into that padded cell. But none of that really excuses me. In my ignorance I had helped kill a guy, plain and simple. And me and the others had done it in, of all places, a hospital. I thought back on the incident with Gunny and Captain Quarter saying, "We don't kill our patients." He was wrong. We had definitely killed *this* patient.

Twice patients had almost killed me. Now a patient I considered a friend might have lived had I insisted on going to town with him; and I had a hand in killing a French sailor. Death was all around, and we weren't even in a war. Worse: it didn't seem to matter. Having once been screwed by The Navy Way, I had now profited from it. In this case it meant not the right way or the wrong way but look the other way.

I was glad not to be in trouble, but I would feel bad about Jonathan and Jean Pierre for a long, long time. Still do.

The Faggots and the Cardinal

———— ⚓ ————

We always had a few gay patients on the locked ward—only we didn't call them "gay," we called them "faggots"; sometimes "fags" for short, but usually "faggots." So, all we basically had to work with wordwise on N-2 were "homosexual" and "faggot." It said "homosexual" on patients' charts, but "faggot" was what we medics and even Captain Quarter usually employed. None of us working on N-2 back then had ever heard the word "gay" used for homosexuals. I've learned since that it existed, that it was used by some gays in America, but our gay Navy and Marine patients didn't use it, and "faggots" sounded friendlier than "homosexual," like a nickname. "Homosexual" sounded clinical, and the faggots seemed to prefer "faggot."

One of them said to me, "I may be a faggot, but I'm no homosexual." I kinda knew what he meant. "Homosexual" sounded like that's what you were—*all* that you were—24/7. "Faggot" sounded like a quirk or a twitch or a hobby or some kind of temporary nuttiness you would eventually get over—or so, in my ignorance, I thought.

I gave up using the word "fag" after an experience in Yokosuka buying a camera. Eight bucks in yen for a Ricohflex, a Japanese knockoff of the great German camera, the Rolleiflex. Stepping out of the store I got talking with a British sailor off a ship that had put into the harbor. After inquiring what my duties were on the base, he asked, "Hey, my good man, got a fag?"

"What?!" I exclaimed. I had no idea that for Brits "fag" meant cigarette.

As for "gay," back then, it was just an old-fashioned way of saying happy or lighthearted, as in "I feel gay today." I remember my father years later inveighing against what he considered the word's expropriation by gays. "I have nothing against homosexuals," he said, "but how come they can say they're 'gay' and I can't any more?"

"You can," I replied.

"No," he insisted. "If I say, 'I feel gay' people will think I'm, well, gay." A friend of mine was also incensed about "gay." "How the hell can I now sing that Christmas carol with, 'Don we now our gay apparel?'" he wanted to know. "I don't want to don any gay apparel. What am I, a transvestite?" He was hoping someday they would change the words of the song or the gays would call themselves something else.

As for me, at twenty-one, I simply did not understand gays, faggots, homosexuals or whatever they were to be called. How could you be attracted to boys rather than girls? Until I started working on N-2, I'd never heard of such a thing. I was too busy figuring out girls. Even married, I was still figuring out girls. In fact, since getting married at such an early age I was especially trying to figure out girls.

I had nothing against the gays on our ward. I just thought they were weird, maybe even weirder than the murderers. Murderers I could understand: you got angry enough you killed someone. Heck, I had almost killed Gunny after he had almost killed me. But being attracted to boys instead of girls? That was inconceivable to me at the time. Sometimes I thought the gays had made it up and *that* was their sickness: they *thought* they were gay.

Had I known what most of us know today—that gays are normal, neither better nor worse, just different— I might have, as with Billy Goldsmith, entertained fantasies of helping the gays escape. It's clear to me now that if anyone on N-2 didn't belong there, it was the gays. But where would they have escaped to? They were in a locked ward in a military hospital on a huge United States naval base in the middle of Japan. But looking back I do feel badly about having been part of what kept young men locked up on N-2 who didn't belong there.

The official word on gays on our ward was that they were "sick." And that was considered charitable. Captain Quarter said "the faggots are a disgrace to the Navy," but he was a doctor, so he felt some obligation to "cure them." He would say, "Too bad we don't have electroshock facilities. That would straighten them out."

"How so, Sir? " I asked him.

"Retrofit their brains, Rockhead," he said, taking me into his confidence, for once forgetting that he was a captain and I a lowly hospitalman third class. "Then they might like girls instead of boys and could have a normal life. They'd be grateful, would thank us for it eventually. That's what they do back in the States with a lot of the faggots. Scramble their brains. We're poorly equipped here."

Townsend seemed to be particularly disappointed that we didn't have electroshock therapy available for the gay patients. He said, "The captain's right. I would love to hook those faggots up, plug them into the wall, zap them. Would serve them right, those cocksucking sons of bitches. I could really dig seeing them jumping like fish on hooks. The guy's lying there with something in his mouth to keep him from biting his tongue off and the next minute he's lit up. I saw it in a movie. It was cool."

Wally told me later: "We'd better watch Townsend with the faggots."

"Why?" I asked.

"Because he said yesterday he wouldn't mind getting a blow job from one of them. On night duty, in the head." This was before my incident with Gunny and the rule we then adopted that neither medic on night duty would go anywhere without the other.

"I don't think so," I said. "The faggots hate Townsend."

"Yeah," said Wally, "but you know him. If he wants something he gets it. You can just see him forcing some gay guy to do it, threatening him with something."

"So now we don't just have to watch the patients, we gotta watch Townsend?"

"We always have had to watch Townsend," Wally replied. "He just doesn't give a shit about anything or anybody. Guys like him once lynched guys like me and thought it was funny."

This was 1957. In 1952, the American Psychiatric Association had classified homosexuality as a mental illness in need of treatment. Homosexuals weren't exactly perverts any more, they were mentally ill. Stuff about being too close to their mothers, trouble with their fathers.

Officially, whether the gays were sick or not, the Uniform Code of Military Justice considered homosexuals criminals and, when our gays left N-2, many were court-martialed and sent to federal prison for a couple of years, usually Leavenworth, before receiving their dishonorable discharges. But if they hadn't been caught in the act, just admitted to being homosexual, they wouldn't go to jail; they would just get kicked out of the military and receive undesirable discharges. Apparently "undesirable" wasn't as bad as "dishonorable."

The Navy wasn't that different from the rest of America. As late as 1961, homosexual acts were crimes in all fifty states. Gays didn't just get a hard time; they got arrested. In 1956, while working on Blueberry Hill, I read a *Time* magazine article in which a psychiatrist opined that ninety percent of homosexuals could be "cured" through psychotherapy. It was the least America could do for them, he said, because "there are no happy homosexuals." That was definitely how Captain Quarter looked at it, except that he also didn't want the gays, happy or not, contaminating his precious Navy.

At least N-2 was better than the Middle Ages. A book in the base library said gays were burned at the stake as heretics. The authorities used only a couple of faggots of wood, didn't burn them, toasted them slowly, wanted them to suffer as long as possible. The condemned gays had to carry those faggots of wood to the stake. That's probably why gays have been called "faggots" this book suggested.

On N-2 we medics never thought of any of this stuff. Homosexuals were the pariahs of the ward, the one group everyone looked down on. There was a patient who was for a long time on one of the medical wards before joining us, a marine. He had tried to kill himself, we were told, because his buddies had said he was a faggot. Shooting himself in the head, he had managed to only blind himself. The bullet had passed straight through the middle of his head taking out both optic nerves but apparently doing little significant damage to his brain.

Before this patient came to N-2 Kreeg had said, "You've gotta go see this guy, Rock. You won't believe it. Shoots himself in the head and he can talk." So one day when I was off duty, I went by the ward where this guy was the only patient. It was the same ward where I had been forced to babysit Billy Goldsmith. The guy looked horrible. His head was swollen to the size of a basketball and was purple in color. When he was first admitted to the hospital the medics on his ward had taken bets on whether he would survive. Talk about conflict of interest. I wondered whether those who bet he would die were entirely committed to his survival.

When he could walk and needed only light medical care and his head had become almost normal looking— mostly just the entry and exit scars—the guy was admitted to N-2. We weren't sure how to classify him, with the faggots or the suicides? Maybe both.

Not being able to see, this guy required lots of care. He was always crashing into things. His presence occasioned more than a few bad jokes from other patients about how homosexuality, not just jerking off, can make you blind.

We had other homosexual patients who were marines, in fact a disproportionate number. We only had three or four gay patients at a time, obviously not a big enough sample to judge, but marine homosexuals seemed to question the stereotype that there are more gays in the

Navy than in any of the other military services. This is something I heard from the moment I entered the Navy. "Watch out," an old friend wrote me in boot camp when he learned I had been inducted into the Navy instead of the Army. "Lots of faggots in the Navy. Guys get aboard ships and, with no women around, they start having at each other." Townsend confirmed this view by saying, "That's one reason I'm glad I have shore duty. On a ship everyone tries to fuck you up the ass when your back is turned."

I talked about this years later with a British friend. He spoke of an old saying about the British Navy, that it "runs on rum and buggery." And, he added, when Winston Churchill took over as First Lord of the Admiralty the first time, in 1911, he responded to a senior naval officer who insisted one of his proposals was "against naval tradition" by saying, "Don't talk to me about naval tradition. It's nothing but rum, sodomy, and the lash."

This myth of a disproportionate number of gays in navies—as far as I know it *is* a myth—is supported by perceptions of Navy uniforms. This was even truer when the thirteen button pants were in vogue in the American Navy, but even I heard wiseguy comments on how Navy guys wore tight pants to show off their asses.

Besides the tight pants, there were the tops we wore that some people considered "kinda girly." This was supported by the fact that it was sometimes referred to as "a blouse" and that it had a feminine flourish of a flap hanging down the back and that women loved to wear Navy tops.

Of course, today we might argue that men unafraid to appear in uniforms that have a softer quality are more comfortable with their masculinity. And we would probably ascribe the disproportionate number of gay marines among the population on N-2 to the super macho character of marines. But these thoughts never occurred to me, nor I suspect, to anyone else working on N-2. There were "real men" and there were faggots, and that's all we knew back then.

An important event took place on the ward that, as it turned out, especially involved the gays. Word arrived that Francis Spellman, the New York cardinal, was coming to Yokosuka Naval base and would be visiting the hospital. Spellman, we were told, had an extra title, "Vicar of the Orient," and, periodically, he visited the major United States military bases in the Far East. Spellman would be visiting our ward, and everyone was uptight about just how to receive him.

Captain Quarter was especially concerned. Whether it had anything to do with him being Catholic, I didn't know. When the date of the Cardinal's visit approached, Quarter insisted that our ward be scrubbed and dusted and that anything that could shine be shined. There were brass doorknobs, so, when not busy with patients, we shined them. There were some brass doorstops and door kick plates, so we shined them too. They were doing the same up on N-1.

Captain Quarter called separate meetings of the staffs of both wards the day before Spellman was expected. He was especially concerned about N-2. "Okay," he said to our staff, "this is what we do. Before the cardinal arrives I want every patient standing by his rack. Stand the catatonics up, and tie them to their racks with a couple of bathrobe belts each. There's also what you guys call 'the whackjobs' to worry about. We don't want them screaming or drooling when the cardinal comes by.

Nurse Kelly will give each of them a shot of Thorazine an hour before the cardinal arrives. Better tie them to their racks too so they don't fall over asleep. A shot of Thorazine for the murderers too. Tell the suicides with bandages to keep their hands behind their backs. We don't want the cardinal seeing that. As he passes through the ward Commander Robinson and I will walk on either side of him and I'd like one of you medics in front of him and one behind. Security. We've got to make sure nobody bothers the cardinal. Is this understood?"

"Yes, Sir," we all said.

"What about the faggots?" Townsend asked.

"I haven't decided yet what to do about them," Quarter said.

It was exciting. A cardinal was coming to our ward, and not just any cardinal: the senior American cardinal, a man considered by many only second in power to the pope. Indeed, a book about him would appear with the title, *The American Pope*. You didn't have to be Catholic to appreciate that a powerful figure would be visiting us, a "celebrity." It made all of us on staff feel important.

Since I was from New York, I was familiar with Cardinal Spellman from regular pictures in the newspapers. Also, as he had been making his way around U.S. bases in the Far East, pictures were daily appearing of him in the *Stars and Stripes* military newspaper. He was short, round, had a cherubic-like pink face, and he looked incredibly clean.

On the day of his visit, we medics had just managed to get all of the N-2 patients lined up properly when we received word by telephone that the cardinal had arrived on N-1 and would be coming down in minutes to N-2.

Then the ward phone rang again. Kreeg answered it and said, "It's for you Rock. It's Captain Quarter."

Oh shit, I thought. *What have I done now?*

But it wasn't something I'd done; it was something Quarter wanted me to do.

"Rockland," he whispered, one of the few times he got my name straight, maybe because he wanted something, "I've finally decided what to do about the faggots. I want you to take them out into the back yard and play basketball with them. I don't want the cardinal knowing we have such people on our ward."

Quarter wasn't worried about the Cardinal knowing about the murderers, but he *was* worried about the faggots.

"But, Sir," I protested, "I was looking forward to seeing the cardinal. I've never met a cardinal before."

Quarter answered me brusquely: "You're Jewish. You don't need to meet the cardinal."

"But what about the faggots, Sir? I think O'Brien and Garcia are Catholics. Surely they should meet the cardinal. How would he even know they're faggots?"

"He's a cardinal; he'd know," Quarter said. "I don't have time to talk about this. Somebody's got to get the faggots off the ward and it might as well be you."

"But…"

"Look," Quarter hissed, "this is a direct order: get the faggots off the ward and do it now!"

So that's what I did. I got the basketball out of the file cabinet in one of the shrinks' offices and called the names of the faggots and told them they were to follow me outside.

They were outraged. "We want to see the cardinal. How come everyone gets to see the cardinal but us?"

I had no answer for them. I was angry enough that I wouldn't get to see the cardinal. There were four gays with me, in pajamas and slippers, one of them the blind guy, assuming he was gay. He wouldn't be much good in the basketball game, so, after guiding him outside, I stationed him at the side of the court on the strip of soil that surrounded the paving. A few weeks before I had planted flowers in the dirt, using seeds purchased at the base PX, thinking it might make things prettier, a little less institutional. But I hadn't kept up with the watering. Weeds had taken over, and my little garden was now a mess, though maybe a little better than just dirt.

The gays and I were still angry that Quarter had sent us outside, but we got a decent basketball game going, two on two. My team had a certain advantage because I wasn't wearing slippers. We were ahead 8-4 when the back door of the ward opened and Kreeg called out: "The cardinal's gone. You can come in now."

I later learned that the cardinal had passed rapidly through the ward blessing everyone. He hadn't been in the ward more than five minutes. Captain Quarter made a point of thanking me for "making sure Cardinal Spellman hadn't been exposed to elements on N-2 we'd just as soon he didn't know about." That was small compensation, but it made me feel a little better.

It would be decades before I learned the truth about Spellman. Magazine stories reported that he had routinely preyed upon young priests, who knew that their progress through church ranks depended on their going along with the cardinal and his habits. He also carried on with chorus boys on Broadway, sending his official limo at night to pick them up after their shows ended and bringing them to the rectory alongside St. Patrick's Cathedral on 5th Avenue in New York City. One journalist wrote that Spellman was "one of the most notorious, powerful, and sexually voracious homosexuals in American Catholic Church history."

Working on N-2 I never thought of such things. In those days it was unthinkable that a priest, much less a cardinal, would be carrying on in this fashion while persecuting homosexuals every chance he got. Now we're used to the idea—and much more.

It was certainly not one of the key events in my life, and it's one I'm certainly not proud of, but I guess I do have the distinction of being *the* United States Navy medic who protected the famous Francis Cardinal Spellman from "exposure" to the gay guys on ward N-2 in the naval hospital at Yokosuka, Japan in 1957. In retrospect, the gay guys on our ward probably needed more protection from the cardinal than he did from them.

Socks

There was another class of patients on N-2 who, unlike the homosexuals, might have actually profited from electroshock therapy, especially at a time when anti-depressants were in their infancy and few understood depression—that it is usually a chemical imbalance and so might be successfully treated with chemicals. But the catatonics were beyond depression. They were just not there. Something had so frightened them that they had retreated into nothingness where they couldn't be hurt any more. It was pitiful to see young men so disabled. And there was no war. Still, something had traumatized them; they were the living dead.

The catatonics took up a considerable amount of our time. They had to be fed and washed and sometimes you had to hold their dicks for them while they peed, so maybe we medics in psychiatric were "pecker checkers" after all—but of a different kind than those who gave shots for the clap. I didn't like holding some guy's dick for him. But you had to do it. Otherwise, the urine might mostly end up inside their pajamas because they didn't hold their own dicks. But anything was better than when they shit themselves. That was the worst. Some of the cats shit themselves regularly. I knew they were mentally ill, but I still hated them when they shit themselves.

You couldn't talk with the cats. You could have a conversation with a murderer—sometimes a really interesting conversation—especially about who they'd killed and why and how they felt about it. Some of the murderers actually seemed like nice guys. And you could obviously have interesting talks with the suicides and the faggots and even the looneys during their brief lucid periods, but you couldn't do anything with a catatonic other than take care of him as if he was an infant.

We kept the catatonics who shit themselves regularly in adult diapers. We had to get these on special order stateside and were always running out of them. This was before Pampers or Depends and before diapers could be attached with Velcro or adhesive tabs. Mostly what we had were large cloth diapers, and we kept the dirty ones in a big bucket out in the recreation yard and sent them to a Japanese laundry in Yokosuka every few days.

You had to attach the diapers with big safety pins. I always hated the pin part. I was scared of sticking a cat with a pin or that, later on, a pin would open by itself and stab the guy and it would be my fault. These pins could do a lot of damage, and the catatonics might never tell you if a pin opened up and was stabbing them because they never told you anything.

Generally, they didn't have to tell you anything when they shit themselves because you could smell it throughout the ward and just follow your nose until you located the right cat. Or one of the other patients would complain, say, "What's the matter with you pecker check-

ers? This guy's shit himself. Do somethin' for crissake! I
may be a nutcase, but my nose still works."

I sometimes thought, *Why should I be changing and
cleaning the cats? We've got murderers in here. Why couldn't
they start serving their sentence right now by cleaning and
changing the cats? It was the least they could do.*

But we pecker checkers were the ones who cleaned
the shit, and we hadn't done anything to merit such
"punishment." Often, when a cat shat himself, we'd argue
about whose turn it was to clean him. Townsend was always trying to get out of it. "Your turn, Rock," he'd say,
even when it wasn't. Finally, Kreeg made a chart so there
would be no arguments about whose turn it was. You
cleaned a cat and put a check next to your name and the
date and hour and the cat's name. But Townsend would
argue even when it was clearly his turn, right there on the
chart.

When you diapered a cat you put rubber pants on
top of the diaper, same as a baby. If you took a catatonic down to the head to pee, you'd have to pull down his
pajama bottoms, pull down his rubber pants, detach the
safety pins and pray you could get this all done before
he started squirting. Once a catatonic peed all over the
front of my uniform. I was pissed on and pissed off. I
went back to the barracks to shower and change.

Most of the catatonics were with us for a month or
two and, if they showed no improvement, were air evacuated back to the U.S. directly into VA hospital mental
wards. I wondered whether they ever got out of there and
had a normal life. Kreeg told me about one cat, before I
arrived on the ward, who came out of it, was soon par-
ticipating in group therapy sessions, moved to the open
ward, and, finally, actually returned to duty, one of the

ward's few success stories. So there remained some hope for the cats.

I think many of us—well, maybe not Townsend—had a desire to help pull a cat out of his zombie state, do something meaningful. I didn't feel that desire often because there was so much to do for the cats. Usually, I just cursed them under my breath, especially when one of them had shit himself and it was my turn. But between such incidents, a bit of idealism—the thought that you might help bring a cat back to the world—returned.

There was one kid I was particularly moved to help. His name was Andrew. He was a marine who, it said in his chart, may have been beaten up regularly by the guys in his unit. There was also the suggestion in his chart that he might have been raped by the same guys. But there was no cause of action because Andrew had never complained to his commanding officer. He had just become deeply depressed and then non-functional. Now he wasn't in any kind of state where he *could* complain.

There was no suggestion in his chart that Andrew was homosexual. He had piercing blue eyes with jet black hair and, even in his zombie state, was handsome to the point of being pretty. You could see where some of the shaved head toughs in the Marines might have, at the least, picked on him, called him a pussy, things like that.

Andrew showed no sign of coming out of his vegetative state. He just sat there all day with a blank expression on his face. I couldn't help liking the kid—partly because he was the only cat who rarely shit himself, so it was easier to think of him as a human being in deep trouble and less just a bother. In fact, you could tell when he needed to shit because he started making sounds like "Nnnnnn, Nnnnnn, Nnnnnn" and, when you heard that you hustled him down to the head. The fact that he could even do that was a sign there was hope for him.

Andrew became something of a project of mine. I concentrated on him when I had time and did my darnedest to help him. I kept thinking that if I could get Andrew to do one thing, say one thing, he'd be on his way back and maybe he'd keep coming—his fuses screwed back in, his wiring connected and sparking. If I could only get him to do or say one thing. That's all I wanted. But if I was to accomplish that it had to be quick: I had only five weeks left in Yokosuka.

But my efforts with Andrew were halted when I got sick. I had come down with a wretched cold—or so it seemed. A doctor elsewhere in the hospital said it was the flu and perhaps because we were in Asia, "the Asian flu," a serious variety. Whatever it was, it knocked me on my ass. It wasn't the sneezing so much; in fact that had stopped before I saw the doctor. I was simply exhausted. It was as if I had been bitten by a Tsetse fly; all I wanted to do was sleep.

I asked Captain Quarter if I could take a few days off, just rest in the barracks, but he said, "This is the Navy. You're well enough for duty or you're in the hospital. Otherwise, you're AWOL." There it was again: "the right way, the wrong way, and the Navy Way." It seemed ridiculous to me. I didn't need to be in the hospital; I just needed to rest. But it was the hospital or working on the ward, so I went to Admissions and got myself checked in.

The guys in Admissions gave me a hard time. "*Malingering* is what we call this in the Navy, Rockland," they said.

"Yeah, well thanks," I said, too exhausted to reply more amply. Just making it down to Admissions had been difficult. I didn't resist when the guys in Admissions insisted I climb aboard a gurney. "Only way you can be admitted," they said. "Rules." I was so tired I didn't mind getting a free ride to the ward they were putting me on, not have to walk there. I assured Admissions that I didn't need to be restrained on the gurney. "Rules," they said again and tied me down. "Besides, you're from N-2. You might go crazy on us," they said, laughing. I hoped that, en route, we didn't run into medics from other wards. They would probably think that, like Jerry Simon, another guy from psychiatric had flipped out.

I was put into a bed on one of the medical wards and lay around waiting for my strength to return. It was weird being a patient in my own hospital.

The corpsmen on this ward, with nothing to do since I was their only patient and needed only bed rest, played cards all day—poker, with big pots of money. I got up once and asked to be dealt in but they said, "You're a fucking patient. Get back in bed." Even though I was a medic just like them, now I was a patient, a lower form of life. None of them even wanted to talk to me. And, besides, I was from Blueberry Hill and, therefore, probably half crazy or, at least, not to be taken seriously.

I was bored. I got hold of some books and magazines, but I've never been able to read in bed for long without falling asleep, and with the exhaustion of the Asian flu even more so. So I'd read a bit and sleep, read some more and sleep. I did get a little hobby going. I started a countdown on a piece of cardboard, putting a line for each day closer to leaving the Navy, celebrating when a unit of five days was completed and I could put a horizontal through four verticals.

I'd have liked it if my colleagues from N-2 had come by when they were off duty to have someone to talk to, even Townsend. Wally Barker did come by once, but it was to say goodbye. It was his last day on N-2. He was being transferred to the naval hospital at San Diego, California for a year or so and then intended to go back to college. He was hoping to become a doctor.

"Didn't you get enough of 'medicine' on N-2?" I asked.

Wally laughed. "What we do on N-2 isn't medicine," he said. "We just try not to fuck up too badly."

"Roger that," I said.

I was sad to see Wally go. He was a good kid, and we had experienced two near death experiences together. We corresponded a bit after he left and after I also returned to the States—postcards, holiday cards—things like that. But our contacts petered out and, eventually, just ended. Recently, I tried to find Wally to ask if, after all these years, he would read this book and give me his reactions—did he remember things as I did?—but I couldn't find him. I thought maybe the Navy might know something—he had stayed in the Reserves or something—but they knew nothing of his whereabouts or even whether he was alive. I tried all the search engines—Google and the like—but no dice. I do hope Wally Barker is alive somewhere and will read this book. And I do hope that he became a doctor. He would have been a good one.

Three weeks before I was scheduled to leave Japan my strength and energy had returned, so I went back to work on N-2, continuing to mark off the days on that piece of cardboard. Kreeg and Townsend were still there, and a new guy I never got to know who had replaced

Wally. Neither Kreeg nor Townsend asked how I felt. I was just back on the job.

Also, I was a "short-timer," and no one in the Navy cares about you once you're a short-timer. You're about to leave, so everybody wants to forget about you already. The people I had felt closest to on N-2—besides Wally Barker, of course—were Billy Goldsmith, the razor blade eater, my one time colleague, Jerry Simon, and Jonathan Shelby, but these three friendships had all ended in disaster. I didn't even want to think about Jonathan because then I'd have been forced to remember the pathologist sawing off the top of his head and yanking his face down inside out.

All Townsend had to say about my leaving soon was, "Get some American pussy for me when you get stateside." I didn't bother to remind him that I was married and wondered whether my wife counted as "American pussy" in Townsend's estimation.

Kreeg did seem to care a little. "Send me a postcard, Rock," he said. I did, and he sent me one back with a picture of the House of the Ten Thousand Flowers, but that was the end of it. Kreeg was regular Navy and, after I got discharged, I was a civilian, a different species. Deep down, the glue of our relationship was N-2, and when that was gone communication went with it.

Kreeg did say one day, "I'll bet you miss it sometimes—the Navy, this ward." He was wrong. I have never missed either for an instant. Or so I tell myself.

I was glad that Andrew the catatonic was still on the ward so, in my remaining weeks, I resumed my project with him. I would talk to him while I was feeding or dressing him. A one way conversation can get old fast, but with Andrew I kept at it. Maybe I could reach him, even if just a little bit. I would ask him questions and then answer them myself. I thought somewhere in there he might be hearing me and could be slowly coaxed back into the world.

I thought that if I could get him to do one thing on his own it would be a good start. What would be the easiest? His socks. If I could get Andrew to put on his socks it would mean that somewhere inside he had heard "sock" and knew what it meant and even, perhaps, knew what to do with it. If I could then get him to put on one sock, I could probably get him to put on the other. Then we could move to his slippers. And on from there: going to the bathroom himself, feeding himself, walking, talking. I kept telling myself that if I concentrated hard enough on it I'd have him on the road back to human.

But I had to be patient, take it slow—even though I had so little time. Just one thing, anything, would be a start.

So I took to saying "socks" out loud as I put on his socks. "Socks," I'd say holding up one of the socks in front of his eyes, "Socks." It was like teaching a baby to say his first word.

Maybe five days went by with me saying "socks" over and over—and feeling a little foolish all the while. Like I was obsessed with socks. Townsend thought I had lost it. "What are you mumbling about to that kid?" he would say. "What's with the 'socks' thing? You sound like a fucking Section 8 yourself, Rock. You ought to check yourself in here."

One day when I was saying "socks" over and over, Andrew himself whispered it, like a question. "Socks?"

"Yes!" I shouted, exultant. I tried to calm down, didn't want to startle him, didn't want to get him off the path we had started down. He was launched. But I had to remember: "Slow, Michael, slow." Get his saying "socks" established and go on from there.

The next day I continued saying "socks" over and over and every once in a while Andrew would say it too, and without the question mark. I was happy, proud even. He was like my little son who had just learned to say "Daddy." I had a million routine things to do with the other patients, but there was joy in Andrew saying "Socks."

Each morning after that I would add something. For a while, as I put on one sock, I would say "Left sock." Then I started doing the same with "right sock." Then I would say "Left sock, right sock." It sounded a little like a Dr. Seuss' story, but I wanted to make sure Andrew knew there were two socks and that one went on his left foot, one on his right. I wanted him to digest that concept. I was so intent on the project with Andrew that I asked Kreeg and the p.m. crew if I might remain in the ward for an hour or so after we were relieved to work exclusively with Andrew.

"Be our guest," they all said, though Kreeg warned me that all I might get out of this volunteering was frustration and heartache. "A long time ago I tried to do something like this," he said, "but it was a bust. Now I just do my job."

"Haven't you yet learned what "N.A.V.Y." stands for, Rock?" he continued. "Never Again Volunteer Yourself."

The next day Andrew said "left sock" without the question. And a few minutes later he said "right sock." It was working. I was having an effect on him. He still never said anything at the morning group therapy sessions nor did the flat expression on his face change, but he had begun his ascent from the depths, and I was the one bringing him up. When the canteen cart came on the ward at 9 o'clock that evening I bought Andrew a Snickers bar as a kind of reward.

It was like giving a dog a treat because he'd done something right. I fed it to him but, at one point he took it out of my hand, looked at it quizzically, and took a bite by himself. That was another plus. This was the first time he had fed himself anything. The next time he said "left sock, right sock" I got him another candy bar. He held it in his hand, uncertain what to do with it, but when I unwrapped it he reached out and took it from me and ate the whole thing himself.

He got it all over his face and sat there with a chocolate beard and mustache, until I got some damp paper towels from the head and cleaned his face. Then he did something I hadn't ever seen him do before: he smiled. It was a faint smile, but it was still a smile. I smiled back and he looked at me, a bit startled, but then seemed to smile again. He trusted me.

I wondered whether he was ready to put on his socks. The next day I handed him the socks but he just held them in his hand and looked at them. Then he looked down at his feet. "Yes," I said, "yes." He was thinking about it, but he didn't do anything, just held the socks and looked at his feet. He couldn't seem to completely connect the socks with his feet. Finally, I took the socks back from him and put them on him.

It went on like this for another day or so. Although I didn't want to rush things I looked at Andrew's chart and discovered that he was due for air evacuation back to the States the day before I was to leave. I had only five more days. I was determined to have Andrew putting on his socks before he left. I owed that to myself as much as to him.

I kept handing him his socks, but now I would also say, "Andrew, put on your socks." He would look at me with an almost pleading look in his eyes, but he didn't say anything and made no move to put on his socks. But I thought the pleading look was a plus. It meant that he wanted to put on his socks but didn't know how. His brain, his hands, and his feet were still all separate, un-connected, or were connected by such thin wires that they carried just a trickle of current. But his face was be-coming more animated with each passing day. The total flatness was gone. There was a hint of a smile. It was as if some light was on in his house; not all of the lights yet, just one up in the attic, but maybe I could help him turn on others.

There were now only three days until he would be air evacuated back to the U.S., and my own tour of duty was quickly coming to a conclusion too. I was deter-mined that, before Andrew left, I'd have him putting on his socks, so I kept saying, "Come on, Andrew, put on your socks," but he just looked at me, and sometimes he would smile, but he didn't put on his socks.

Now there were only two days. I did my best not to show my frustration but inside I was feeling, "Goddamn it, Andrew, put on your fucking socks."

On his last day on the ward something happened that hadn't happened before. I told him that this was his last day on N-2 and that I hoped, as a favor to me, he would put on his socks.

He seemed to be listening to me intently. His eyes were bright, his skin shiny with life. It was as if his blood, which had only circulated sufficiently to keep him alive, was now speedily coursing through his body. His face glowed. More lights were coming on. He looked like a different person.

"Come on, Andrew," I said, "put on your socks. Do it for me, please."

This time when I held out the socks he met me half way and took them out of my hands. He placed one sock on the floor next to his right foot and the other next to his left foot. I was excited.

Then he asked me a question I'll never forget: "Which one first?" They were his only words in those weeks besides "socks" and "right sock, left sock." I loved hearing those three beautiful words, "Which one first?"

Then I blew it. Casually, I said, "Doesn't matter. You decide."

He pondered that for a moment and then a look I can only describe as an expression of horror swept across his face. And then it went completely flat again, all the expression swept from it in a flash. Every light went out.

In my haste I had skipped a step. All he was ready for then was for me to tell him which sock to put on first. He wasn't ready to make a decision between left and right. If I had told him which to put on first he would have been okay; he would have done it. But I had given him two things to do: not only put on a sock but, much more difficult for him, decide which one to put on first.

There are those among us who follow a ritual in putting on socks. We always put on the left one first, then the right—or the other way around. We're not even conscious of making that choice; we just do it. Some of us are even afraid to do otherwise, think bad things will happen if we put the wrong sock on first; we'll lose the ball game, the evil eye will be upon us.

Andrew had wanted me to tell him which sock to put on first and, like a fool, I had given him freedom of choice—something he wasn't ready for yet. Freedom is tricky. None would admit it, but there's often comfort in being told what to do rather than being given a choice. That's why people join cults: some guru tells them exactly what to do.

There's a scene in the movie *Moscow on the Hudson* where the character played by Robin Williams, a Soviet musician who defects in New York City, starts hyperventilating and flips out when he goes into a supermarket to buy some coffee. Standing in the coffee aisle he contemplates eighty different brands of coffee and goes nuts. He was used to things in the Soviet Union where, when there was coffee at the GUM store, and you waited on line all day, they finally handed you, if you were lucky, a paper bag with coffee in it—no brands, no decaf and regular, no instant or crystals or ground: just coffee. The Williams character was evacuated from the supermarket to a hospital in serious condition. Choice, freedom, nearly killed him.

That was my mistake with Andrew: I put him in a position where he had to decide something. I drove him back into being a vegetable because he couldn't yet tolerate choice. Sure, there was no reason in the world why putting on one sock first made more sense than putting on the other first. But stressful complexity of some sort had originally sent Andrew into the safety of catatonia, and now I had driven him right back there. When I said it didn't matter which sock he put on first he had sunk like a stone.

The next day they came for Andrew. He was going to be put on a hospital plane with patients collected from all over Japan and Korea. A medic came for him, and he left in his pajamas and bathrobe. I stood by the door of N-2 as he stumbled towards it. I hoped for a sign of recognition, something, anything as testimony to what he and I had tried to do together. But his face was flat, his eyes vacant as he passed me. He never looked at me.

I had a great sense of loss. Though we were about the same age, he had been like a son to me. I had cared about him, had a great deal invested in him, and I had failed.

Townsend, who had observed my efforts with Andrew over the previous weeks and saw the sadness on my face now, said, "Rock, you are a sorry motherfucker." How I wish there had been someone with whom I could share my sorrow about Andrew, but Townsend's "sorry" was the only thing I was going to get.

Epilogue

When I left the Navy I threw the sea bag with all my Navy clothes into a Goodwill Industries depository. In the Seventies bell bottom pants were all the rage, but I didn't wear them because they reminded me of the Navy. Later, I was invited to join The Navy League, old salts who get together to reminisce about their Navy days, I said, "You gotta be kidding." The last thing I wanted to reminisce about was my Navy days.

Yet here I've gone and written a whole book about them, so perhaps I am a bit nostalgic about the Navy, especially for Ward N-2 at the Yokosuka Naval Hospital despite all its horrors. Maybe Jimmy Kreeg was partly right when he said, "I'll bet you miss it sometimes—the Navy, this ward." I don't know that I've ever missed it as such. However, I am a bit grateful to the Navy that during those two years I may have experienced as many strange things as in the rest of my life put together.

Many years after my Navy service I was back in Japan on a lecture trip sponsored by our embassy in Tokyo and discovered a country I did not know. The Third World country I was familiar with was gone.

Japan was dramatically more modern than the United States. Trains moving at two hundred miles an hour crisscrossed the country. Hotels were so advanced you could accomplish virtually anything just by pushing a few buttons. My rooms seemed as much like spaceships as living quarters. The food was nothing short of magnificent. And everything was fiercely expensive.

But it was the people who most surprised me. The Japanese seemed to be a foot taller, especially the young women—though that was partly due to the platform heels they wore as they swung down the sidewalk in Tokyo, every last one of them with a cell phone glued to her ear. Their mothers and grandmothers had been meek little things.

The girls on the Tokyo sidewalks were flirtatious, even brash. They all spoke passable English and seemed to be into hip hop and goth. They wore black. Many of them had dyed their hair chartreuse or fuchsia.

"Where you from?" they asked

"New Jersey," I replied

"Ah, so," they said, "Springsteen, Sopranos, New Jersey Turnpike." Those girls seemed to have a keen interest in New Jersey culture.

My hosts during the lecture trip were usually Japanese university professors, all of whom spoke passable English. When we first met everyone bowed non-stop. At least that hadn't changed; my lower back was killing me. Once, with a group of professors I tried out my landlord story on them, wondering how they would react. Almost in unison they laughed hysterically, were doubled over in mirth. I couldn't tell whether they were laughing because they found the story ridiculous or all too familiar. In any case, I was left with no new insights into the behavior of my Japanese landlord long ago.

On a day when I had only an early morning lecture I left Tokyo by train for Yokosuka. When I got off the gleaming new train, I didn't recognize anything about the city. It was no longer a series of rickety structures; everything was shiny and modern. There was a large Nissan plant that claimed to produce one car per minute. When I worked on the base virtually no one in Japan owned a car. Now everyone seemed to be whizzing by in late model cars on major thoroughfares and highways that bisected the city.

Yokosuka even had skyscrapers and a beautiful Museum of Art. There was also a lovely park. Everyone in the streets was well dressed, prosperous looking. I wondered if the House of Ten Thousand Flowers still existed. If it did, I imagined a girl would now cost more like two hundred instead of two dollars.

The U.S. Naval Base was still there, looking less grimly grey than what I remembered. But they wouldn't let me in. "Hey," I told the MPs at the main gate, "I once worked here." That carried no weight with them. "Sorry, Sir," they said, "American civilians are not allowed to come on the base." Well, at least they said "Sir." Nobody in uniform had ever called me "Sir" when I was in the Navy. "Fuckface," "Scumbag," "Asshole"—things like that—but never "Sir."

Luckily, an officer approached and asked what the problem was. When I told him that I was in Japan on a State Department lecture trip, he went to make a phone call—probably to the Embassy in Tokyo to check on me—and, after asking me to leave my passport with the

MP's, he said he had some free time and could take me around the base.

What I most wanted to see was whether my old hospital building was still there. I knew that a new hospital had been built in the early 1980s, and, I was told, the psychiatric wards were there. But E-22 still stood and was used for such purposes as marriage counseling and treatment for alcoholism. I felt comforted that activities, on an out patient basis, were being carried on in E-22 not entirely unrelated to what I had been involved in so many years before.

But it probably would have been better had I not entered E-22. It looked more or less the same on the outside, as best I remembered it, but I didn't recognize anything inside and found myself lost in a building I once knew so well. There wasn't a trace of that building; no ghosts haunted the place. Especially disconcerting was that I couldn't find where N-2 had been. I was actually happy, after ten confusing minutes, to get out of there and back to my memories.

On another day when I was mostly free I couldn't decide whether to go to Kamakura to see my old friend, The Great Buddha, or to Hayama and search for my house and to see whether my landlord still lived next door. Had I done so, and he was there, ancient by now certainly, I wondered if he would recognize me and immediately swing into his coming over for dinner routine. It would have been worth going to Hayama just for that. It would have been the perfect finale to the shaggy dog story of many years before.

But I figured it was unlikely my landlord was alive and was concerned whether Hayama, like Yokosuka, had been so reconfigured as to be unrecognizable. Could I even find my old house or had it been torn down and replaced by an office building?

So I decided to go to Kamakura which, like Yoko-suka, looked disturbingly different, but at least I found the Great Buddha and soon was standing in front of him. Once again, his eyes and expressionless face interested me, but I wasn't sure now whether what I saw there was enlightenment or simply stoicism. As was the case many years before, I could not decide whether he was exuding love, giving the world the finger, or both.

Also, something had changed in the Buddha's meaning to me. He was now mostly just a big, strange statue. He had been my refuge from the Navy, but he didn't do anything for me now.

About the Author

⚓

MICHAEL AARON ROCKLAND is professor of American studies at Rutgers University. His years in the United States Navy (1955-1957) as a medical corpsman inspired this memoir. It is his fourteenth book.

In his writing, Rockland moves back and forth between memoir, fiction, journalism, and history. Five of his books have won prizes or received similar recognition, including *New York Times'* "Notable Book of the Year" and *Washington Post's* "Fifty Best Books of the Year." A book he co-wrote, *Looking for America on the New Jersey Turnpike*, was chosen by the New Jersey State Library as one of the "Ten Best Books Ever Written on New Jersey or by a New Jerseyan." Two other books received the prize of the New Jersey Studies Alliance.

Rockland has also worked in television and filmmaking and is a regular contributor to several magazines, most regularly *New Jersey Monthly*. He has won five major teaching awards, including the national teaching award in American Studies.

Rockland is happy to receive responses from readers. Please contact him at http://michaelrockland.com/Contact.html.

Also by Michael Aaron Rockland

Stones

A sneaky and beautiful little masterpiece – sneaky because its disarmingly simple premise of a single day spent visiting graves manages somehow to communicate the endless complexity of one Jewish-American family over the span of nearly a century, and beautiful because Michael Rockland tells his story with a generous, generous heart.

—Tom De Haven, author of *It's Superman*

STONES is a novel simultaneously serious and comic. It takes place in one day as its protagonist, Jack Berke, accompanies his aged mother Rachel to visit the family graves in Brooklyn, Queens, and further out on Long Island. As Jack negotiates the congested expressways from cemetery to cemetery, he contemplates the tombstones, the lives of family members who lie under them, the stones that, according to Jewish custom, he places on those tombstones, and the stone that has for a lifetime resided in his own heart.

Available in paperback (ISBN 978-1-60182-300-7) and eBook (ISBN 978-1-60182-301-0).

An American Diplomat in Franco Spain

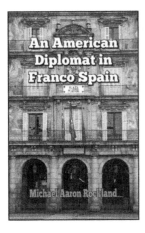

What pleasure it gives me to encounter an American, a former diplomat, who understands so well our country, past and present, and who is equally at home in the world and language of Cervantes as that of Shakespeare.

—Jorge Dezcallar, *Ambassador of Spain to the United States*

AN AMERICAN DIPLOMAT IN FRANCO SPAIN is filled with Michael Aaron Rockland's experiences as a cultural attache at the United States embassy in Madrid, Spain in the 1960s. He captures episodes of historical and cultural significance as he goes about doing his country's business. Some of his stories are quite poignant while others are quite amusing. He shares with his readers how he avoided shaking Francisco Franco's hand, how he spent a day with Martin Luther King in Madrid, how his son was selected to be in the movie Dr. Zhivago, how he came to know several Kennedys, including Senator Edward Kennedy, Pat Lawford Kennedy, and Jackie Kennedy, and how the U.S. accidentally dropped four unarmed hydrogen bombs on Spain. Throughout these stories, Rockland explains Spanish culture, past and present.

Available in paperback (ISBN 978-1-60182-304-5) and eBook ISBN (978-1-60182-305-2).

CPSIA information can be obtained at www.ICGtesting.com
Printed in the USA
LVOW05s1950031014

407175LV00012BA/186/P